"The holy and unhurried spiritual journey will deeply touch hungry souls longing to pull away from the clamoring vicissitudes of life. While mainstream society focuses on busyness and accomplishments, Alan Fadling calls disciples to detach from such overcommitted, narcissistic lifestyles. *A Non-Anxious Life* offers a multiplicity of spiritual practices and paradigms that provide genuine transformation. This book makes a clarion call for the beloved to abide in God's presence. Having a relationship with Jesus, the Prince of Peace, is the essential foundation for spiritual maturation and living an unhurried life."

Barbara L. Peacock, spiritual director and author of *Soul Care in African American Practice*

"I don't often admit the constancy of anxiety in my life—but with Alan Fadling, I think I could risk the honesty. The wisdom of his deeply personal book *A Non-Anxious Life* has been gained through gracious movement toward the trustworthy friendship of Jesus. As Fadling reminds us through Scripture and story, in the company of Christ—and with a vision of his sufficiency and care—we need never be afraid. What simple, freeing news that readers will benefit to learn—and practice."

Jen Pollock Michel, author of *In Good Time* and *A Habit Called Faith*

"Alan Fadling reminds us that 'the peace of Jesus doesn't depend on a stress-free setting.... The peace of Jesus is deep-rooted.' This book was a mirror, reminding me of what I need so consistently but am so often too busy to recognize—the abiding peace of Christ and the liberating power it can have. *A Non-Anxious Life* is a rich, inspiring, and practically helpful book that any and all who wrestle with the frenetic pace of modern life must read."

Jay Kim, pastor and author of *Analog Christian*

"Alan Fadling is a seasoned and wise guide who gently points the longing and unsatisfied heart in a different direction than to the frenetic pace and seductive siren songs of our noisy and anxious culture. Each carefully chosen word reflects a gifted artist of the soul whose insights from Holy Scripture along with contemplative voices from the past, as well as his own transparent spiritual journey, bring renewed peace and hope to any weary soul. I highly recommend this book."

Tom Nelson, president of Made to Flourish and author of *The Flourishing Pastor*

"To be human is to be anxious. It is not a question of if, but in what way are we anxious and how we respond to it. Never before have we been more acquainted with all that is true about this; never before have we been more worried about our worry. But thanks be to God, for our good fortune, into our moment comes *A Non-Anxious Life*, Alan Fadling's superlative offering on what it means to live in the world, practicing becoming the people that Jesus imagines us to become. Vulnerable, accessible, and practical, this volume is timely and filled with great wisdom. Read it and learn to become anxious for nothing, on the way to becoming an outpost of peace in all your life's endeavors."

Curt Thompson, MD, author of *The Soul of Desire* and *The Soul of Shame*

A NON-ANXIOUS *Life*

EXPERIENCING THE PEACE OF GOD'S PRESENCE

ALAN FADLING

An imprint of InterVarsity Press
Downers Grove, Illinois

InterVarsity Press
P.O. Box 1400 | Downers Grove, IL 60515-1426
ivpress.com | email@ivpress.com

InterVarsity Press® is the publishing division of InterVarsity Christian Fellowship/USA®. For more information, visit intervarsity.org.

All Scripture quotations, unless otherwise indicated, are taken from The Holy Bible, New International Version®, NIV®. Copyright © 1973, 1978, 1984, 2011 by Biblica, Inc.™ Used by permission of Zondervan. All rights reserved worldwide. www.zondervan.com. The "NIV" and "New International Version" are trademarks registered in the United States Patent and Trademark Office by Biblica, Inc.™

While any stories in this book are true, some names and identifying information may have been changed to protect the privacy of individuals.

The publisher cannot verify the accuracy or functionality of website URLs used in this book beyond the date of publication.

Cover design: David Fassett
Interior design: Jeanna Wiggins
Cover images: Getty Images: © the_burtons, © by Ruhey, © Kreangagirl

ISBN 978-1-5140-0050-2 (print) | ISBN 978-1-5140-0051-9 (digital)

Printed in the United States of America ∞

Library of Congress Cataloging-in-Publication Data

Names: Fadling, Alan, 1961- author.
Title: A non-anxious life : experiencing the peace of God's presence / Alan
   Fadling.
Description: Downers Grove, IL : IVP Formatio, [2024] | Includes
   bibliographical references.
Identifiers: LCCN 2023030120 (print) | LCCN 2023030121 (ebook) | ISBN
   9781514000502 (print) | ISBN 9781514000519 (digital)
Subjects: LCSH: Anxiety–Religious aspects–Christianity.
Classification: LCC BV4908.5 .F33 2024 (print) | LCC BV4908.5 (ebook) |
   DDC 152.4/6–dc23/eng/20230808
LC record available at https://lccn.loc.gov/2023030120
LC ebook record available at https://lccn.loc.gov/2023030121

31 30 29 28 27 26 25 24 | 12 11 10 9 8 7 6 5 4 3 2 1

To my mother, Shirley Fadling Kipp.

May grace be with us both as we find our way

from unhelpful anxiety to fruitful peace.

I dedicate this book to you in your eighty-third year.

May God's empowering presence,
his measureless generosity,
and his great goodness be with you,
seeking you before ever you seek him.
And may grace bear the fruit of
deep well-being, freedom from anxious care,
and a soul at rest in the presence of
God our Father and the Lord Jesus Christ.
Amen!

CONTENTS

1 Becoming a Master of Anxiety   1

2 Anxiety Isn't for the Birds   16

3 Students Become Mentors   29

4 Gracious Fullness   41

5 Practicing Presence   56

6 Simple Virtues   68

7 Unexpected Paths to Peace   82

8 A Buoyant Life   93

9 Confronting the Giant   106

10 Peace in Troubling Times   122

11 Embodied Peace   136

12 Rhythms of Peace   150

13 Non-Anxious Work   164

14 Becoming a Master of Peace   180

Acknowledgments   197

Appendix A: A Non-Anxious Prayer   199

Appendix B: Group Guide   203

Notes   209

1

BECOMING A MASTER OF ANXIETY

For most of my adult life, I've been a master of anxiety. I'm working to become a master of peace.

Without realizing it, I became a student of anxiety as a child. I grew up in a home with a mom who learned anxiety in a post–World War II midwestern orphanage. From ages four to fourteen, she, together with her older brother and sister, learned the ways of worry. And growing up, I sat at her feet. Am I blaming my mother for my worries? No; I'm no victim. I'm simply telling my story.

We all have our reasons for wrestling with worry or anxiety. But our reasons are not insurmountable. As followers of the Prince of Peace, we can place ourselves at his feet to learn to live in his way of peace. We can learn peace for our hearts and minds, peace in our relationships (as far as it depends on us), peace in our vocational life, and peace in our perspective about the future. This peace is not dependent on things going the way we like. It does not require that everything happen the way we prefer. The way of peace that Jesus leads us into is a way that begins from within us in relationship with him. It does not require peaceful circumstances to survive.

So this book is not a theoretical research project. It isn't a message I'm preparing for others. Writing this book has been a necessary personal quest. Anxiety has, at times, diminished me, hindered me, even paralyzed me—it really has. I'm writing as a fellow student and not a master. I have been on a journey to discover the way of peace.

THE RISE OF ANXIETY

Anxiety has been on the rise for a while. A study by the National Institutes of Health indicates that anxiety steadily increased in the adult population from 2008 to 2018. In that same time frame, anxiety doubled among eighteen- to twenty-five-year-old young adults.[1] But in the first year of the pandemic, the World Health Organization measured a 25 percent increase in anxiety and depression worldwide.[2]

We all had different experiences of anxiety during the global pandemic. My first was sitting on a plane in Delhi, India, in the early morning hours of a mid-February Saturday in 2020. Covid-19 was just beginning to hit our news feeds, but it felt mostly an "out there" issue for me at the time.

As our scheduled departure time came and went, I noticed flight attendants conferencing in the first-class galley. After more than an hour delay, the flight purser announced that there was a passenger with flu-like symptoms whom they were assessing, who needed to be deplaned before we could depart. Anxiety!

We were told that if we brought that passenger with us back to the States, the whole plane load of us would be quarantined for two weeks; the first cruise ship had recently been quarantined in Japan with infected passengers. It took about ninety minutes before they convinced the passenger to deplane, and we finally left the gate. As we taxied toward take-off, an announcement was made, requesting that if there was a doctor on board to make themselves known. We had already left the sick passenger behind. Now what? More anxiety.

Just before we pulled onto the runway to leave, an announcement told us that yet *another* passenger was found to have flu-like symptoms and that we would be returning to the gate. There was an audible gasp from the rest of us. Even more anxiety.

Once we got back to the gate, it didn't take long for this second passenger to do the walk of shame from the back of the plane to the exit. I had needed the restroom for some time, but we'd been told to remain seated. Once the passenger went by and departed, I jumped up and ran into first class for the restroom that I could see was not in use.

While in there, a text notification went off on my smartphone. When I got out of the restroom, I read the text. It essentially said that because of our departure delay, the crew had timed out and would not be able to depart on the flight any longer due to FAA regulations on shift lengths and such. I showed the text to one of the attendants standing there and he looked as concerned as I felt. I went back to my seat and wrestled with what I was going to do in Delhi for twenty-four more hours. I had no local contacts or plans. Still more anxiety.

After about fifteen minutes, an attendant came on to say that if we would be seated immediately, they had been given special permission by the FAA to work a longer than allowed shift and take us home. Finally, after a total delay of three hours, we departed. Nearly twenty-four hours later I arrived home, gave my wife, Gem, a kiss hello, and we both soon found ourselves in bed for the next month with Covid-19.

I began to feel this pandemic crisis emotionally, therefore, a month before what would become a worldwide shutdown. And it began a season in which my anxieties would assail me in new and surprising ways.

WHAT ANXIETY LOOKS LIKE

What I've been learning is that anxiety is a deep-rooted habit that has formed in me over time. It's easy enough to worry about things that feel or look bad to me, but I can also worry when things are going well (*When is all of this finally going to turn bad?* I wonder). Acknowledging the reality of anxiety as a habit has been good news for me. With work, habits can be changed.

The ways in which I have let anxiety malform me can be reformed.

I am not trapped.
I am not hopeless.
I am not helpless.

I have been learning to cultivate perspectives and habits of peace.

I'm learning how to upgrade my internal operating system from anxiety to peace. An operating system is the software that provides a foundation for the basic functions of a computer. Though we are far more complex than a computer, our souls have a sort of operating system as well. Few of us think much about the operating system for our computers. And too few of us think about the ones that run our lives.

Anxiety has too often been my basic way of approaching situations and people. It wasn't as though there was a moment when I sat down and decided that it was the system for me. It was the system I'd received growing up. I've built programs on this foundation that "work," but not very well. Anxiety has proven to be a bad habit of soul hurry that I can unlearn and have been unlearning.

What does this operating system upgrade look like for me?

- It has replaced a tunnel-vision perspective with a more spacious and options-rich one.

- It has replaced an energy-demanding and energy-draining dynamic with one that has proven energy-renewing.

- It has replaced knee-jerk assumptions about my past, present, and future with a freeing vision of many very good options that surround me.

When I call peace an operating system, I'm saying that it is possible to learn to allow peace to be the underlying framework of our lives. Instead of accepting insecurity as my default, I've learned to assume confidence and resourcefulness as my foundation. I've replaced a lot of internalized stress with more inner peace and calm. Peace might even become something unconsciously trusted rather than frantically sought. I've found that while peace is a fruit of the Spirit, anxiety is not. Peace is creative. Anxiety isn't. Peaceful is resourceful, but worry isn't.

I've been discovering that peace isn't hiding from me and playing hard to get. Peace is in me because my very body is a temple of the Holy Spirit. That Spirit bears the fruit of peace from within me. It makes a great deal of difference to remember that I'm living in the Prince of Peace and he is living in me. The peace of God can bubble up from within at any moment and in any place. The sort of peace the world offers is profoundly dependent on optimal conditions and situations.

A lot of my worries are triggered by circumstances. Something happens (or threatens to happen) and anxiety is triggered. I imagine disastrous trajectories inevitably growing out of present dynamics. Anxiety has sometimes felt like my only reasonable option in the face of certain perceived hazards or threats. But I've never regretted upgrading my operating system from anxiety to peace.

I wish that it were a permanent upgrade, but I often have to reboot into this more peaceful way of living. One way I do this is by recalling that the Lord is shepherding me well (Psalm 23:1). What more could I want?

It may not seem realistic to be at peace every moment. I'm not claiming to have arrived in a place where I never feel anxious or worried anymore. We all live real lives with challenges, obstacles, and threats. And anxiety still erupts in me in reaction to unpleasant surprises. When I talk about a non-anxious life, I'm talking about something that can begin *within* us. I've often said that busy is a matter of calendar, and hurry is a matter of soul. In that spirit, anxiety is a result of focusing on our circumstances, and peace is a fruit of focusing on the Prince of Peace, the Shepherd of our souls.

It's been good to remind myself that anxious living isn't a faithful reflection of my present reality in God's good kingdom. Rather than being on the verge of presumed danger, I am in the presence of powerful love. The faithfulness of God-with-me is measureless. My anxiety doesn't take that into account.

And anxiety is not a tone of voice used by the Spirit of God. The voice of anxiety in the back of my head is not the voice of the Spirit's counsel. But sometimes the weight I give that voice might lead someone to think that I'm taking it as a divine word. The way of God is a way of peace. Shalom. Well-being. A life rich with reliable goodness. I can live in peace because I'm in the presence of Peace.

Anxiety is not an especially wonderful counselor. The advice anxiety has given me over the years has not borne good fruit. It has driven me to mindless activity. It has gotten me stuck in narrow, untrue visions of my life. It's been more like a false prophet than a wonderful counselor. It helps when I've downsized anxiety's mentoring role in my life and done what I can to disregard its warnings more often.

My anxiety reminds me of a common experience I have with squirrels when I cycle on local bike trails. I like squirrels, but not along the bike trail. I was cycling the other day when a squirrel darted out in front of me, just missing becoming a squirrel pancake by about twelve inches. In the process, he provoked a jolt of adrenaline in me that felt like anxiety at full volume.

Do these little guys have a death wish? Are they daring one another to jump in front of those big rolling things that race by? I think I know what's happening: they hear me coming and it sounds like danger. In reaction, their little squirrel brain urges them to find safety. Go home! Except that it seems like their home is always on the other side of the bike trail.

So the instinct to race home puts them in more danger than if they took a moment to see what they were hearing and decide on the best course of action. That would be to stay put, but they don't seem to understand that.

My anxiety is a lot like this squirrel instinct. Something shocks me or threatens me, and I go into self-protection mode. "Get safe!" is what my safety-seeking brain cries out. But if I don't take a moment to look around, I may put myself in the way of greater harm by operating in the tunnel of anxiety. I hope I'm smarter than a squirrel.

ANXIETY ZOMBIE

I've had a strange, zombie-like relationship with anxiety. I've been semi-aware of its presence with me, but I've sought to avoid it at the same time. This doesn't make it go away. Anxiety is active, but it isn't alive; it's a kind of living death. It's frantically busy, but not vitally alive.

Too often, my go-to strategy in dealing with anxiety could be summed up in three words: numbing, escaping, and avoiding. Instead of finding true rest amid my anxious feelings, I've escaped through food, drink, or mind-numbing media engagement. I've escaped into my imagination, into endless online journeys, and into familiar video games. I've avoided my life sometimes by over-checking my email and social media, and at the cost of avoiding important work.

If I can resist the temptation to numb, escape, or avoid, it helps because these are counterfeits of peace. Numbing prevents me from feeling the anxiety that is in me. Escaping is an attempt to run away from anxiety. Avoiding is my effort to do an end-run around anxiety. But I can learn to be present to my anxieties in the presence of God. I can feel anxious and learn to not let that drive me to worry.

So when I numb, escape, or avoid, I don't feel my anxiety for a while. But not *feeling* anxious doesn't mean that the roots of anxiety have been addressed. I'm simply numb to them for a while. Numbness and peace don't really feel the same. One is a lack of feeling. The other is a sense of well-being, or being relaxed, or becoming confident.

I choose numbing in my lack of vision for how anxiety might actually be resolved. I prefer to feel numb than to feel anxious. But learning to receive peace is better than not feeling anxiety temporarily. It's hard to be healed of that which I cannot feel.

For example, I often find myself feeling a dull anxiety as I begin a typical workday. I have a nebulous dread that I'm not going to be up to the work that lies ahead. I've too often attended more to the anxiety that whispers its dark insinuations than to the peace of God that is always with me. This is draining. I sometimes feel worn out in seasons with a monotonous schedule, unbroken by outside speaking or travel. Anxiety suggests I'm just about out of gas for the work to which I feel called. And for some reason, I find myself listening to and believing its counsel.

How do I navigate what feels like paralyzing anxiety when I have work that needs to be done? How do I overcome these strong negative feelings? What does the fruitful path forward look like? Is it true that this experience is a necessary weakness so I might grow strong in grace? Is this sort of thing like Paul's thorn in the flesh, or is it something that simply should be resolved through counsel, coaching, or medications?

I've worried a lot. I sometimes worry about how much I worry. Then I worry that I'm worrying about my worries. There are layers of present worry that reinforce layers of ancient worry laid down in my very body. Anxiety is obviously a problem for me.

A VISION OF ANXIETY

For years, the cars Gem and I drove were older models donated to us through the nonprofits in which we served. One day, the red check engine light came on as one of our sons was driving. We took the old car to our mechanic to figure out what was wrong. A few days later, he called to say that he'd run every diagnostic he could think of, but nothing resolved the engine light. His opinion was that the computer itself was malfunctioning, and that replacing it on such an old vehicle was not worth the cost. He recommended that we simply continue driving the car for as long as we'd own it with that light stuck on.

I think the red-light indicator of my own habitual anxiety is like that check engine light. It comes on, often stays on, and warns me of some major problem that may not even exist. It claims to be warning me of a problem, but it may *itself* be the problem.

It's important to notice my anxiety, to discern whether its warnings are helpful, and to respond accordingly. Too often, I assumed my anxiety indicator was an infallible source of truth about my past, present, or future; it often hasn't been.

My anxiety is also like trying to time-travel into my past or my future. Anxiety recalls unpleasant or painful experiences for me to replay, rehearse, and ruminate on. Anxiety paints a dystopian image of what lies ahead of me. Letting anxiety tempt me to time-travel like this isn't productive. The grace of God is available to me now, but anxiety overlooks the present moment. And it can't actually see the future about which it makes such confident proclamations of doom. The future it predicts has rarely been as disastrous as threatened.

Anxiety is never satisfied. If I listen to its frantic warnings, it does not stop there—it finds something else to warn me about. Anxieties followed tend to multiply into more anxiety. Anxiety has not led me to a path of safety and therefore peace. It leads me to fretting and more anxiety. It is not a path of life. It does not bear good fruit in my soul, my relationships, my work, or my leadership.

My anxiety is like buying into a conspiracy theory. Anything that supports the conspiracy is embraced as trustworthy authority; anything that contradicts the conspiracy is rejected as part of the conspiracy. Anxiety flourishes in that kind of insecurity and doubt about the goodness of my path with God.

Non-anxious living is more than dealing with anxious feelings. It's an orientation to life. It's learning to live a life of shalom, of well-being, of healthy rhythms, of cooperation with the kingdom ways of God. I'm seeking to describe a non-anxious life in far broader and more global terms. I've been learning that it is a kind of pace at which I live, and relate, and work.

Now, let me be clear: a non-anxious life is not a life without concerns. It is not a life without difficulties or hardships. It is not a life in which I never feel nervous. A life completely free of cares would be a life in which nothing matters to me. The great commandment is, at its heart, a command to care. It isn't baptized stoicism. It is peaceful caring that is with us in our actual troubles.

I'm grateful for many resources that have helped me with my anxiety. I have benefited from years of psychological therapy. I have done important work with issues that arise in my adult life, rooted in childhood and youth experiences. I've found fruitful freedom from forms of anxiety that used to often overwhelm and even paralyze me. I have recently taken advantage of medication for depression and anxiety. All of this has helped. What I'm exploring in this book is how we might embrace the resources available to us in the peaceful kingdom of God and in the presence of the Prince of Peace.

CONTINUING AS WE BEGAN

In contrast to anxiety is trust or faith. Paul offers this counsel to his friends in Colossae: "So then, just as you received Christ Jesus as Lord, continue to live your lives in him, rooted and built up in him, strengthened in the faith as you were taught, and overflowing with thankfulness" (Colossians 2:6-7). While the language of peace isn't explicitly present, these have been words of wisdom to deepen my experience of peace in the presence of God.

How did I receive Christ Jesus as Lord in my youth? I received Christ like I would receive any gift. I trusted in the generosity of the Father's gift of his Son. There was nothing I could do to make myself deserving of such a gift. I could only welcome divine generosity with open hands.

What has enabled me to find peace in this kingdom counsel has been Paul's little phrase "just as." My continuing journey can be lived in the very same spirit in which I embarked on this journey. I live my life in Christ Jesus as Lord *just as* I received him—still receiving his generous initiative and kind provision.

This has been a grounding and stabilizing reality for me. I'm living my life in response to the kind and lavish work of God in Christ. I've learned to find growing confidence in the life already available to me from God the Father through Christ the Son empowered by the Holy Spirit. Confident trust in this triune communion has deepened my peace. This way of living has caused gratitude to well up in me more often. I am finding this a peaceful way to live even when circumstances tempt me to worry and to be anxious.

My worry is often rooted in trying to manage something that feels unmanageable to me. It helps when I recognize that the One I've come to follow is not overwhelmed by what overwhelms me. I'm ultimately safe in the presence of a very good shepherd. Do I always feel safe? No. Am I never threatened by people or circumstances? That would be nice, but not real. I am safe, though, from ultimate harm. As Julian of Norwich heard in a divine vision during a dark time in human history (disease and war were rampant), "All shall be well"—I'm coming to trust that simple statement as a description of my own present and my own future. And in this I am finding peace.

I think of Jesus' words to Martha, and to us, in Luke 10. He speaks with great compassion to our many worries. He doesn't accuse us, shame us, or condemn us. He seeks to lift our eyes to see his good presence with us to protect our hearts and minds. I think some people imagine that Jesus' repeated "Martha, Martha" is spoken with arms crossed, head shaking, and brows furrowed in disappointment. But I imagine the face of Jesus full of compassion. He is, after all, the Prince of Peace who takes no pleasure in the anxiety of his beloved children.

A FELLOW TRAVELER

I set out to write a book about living a life free of anxiety. Somewhere, in the back of mind, I hoped I'd find a life where I'd never even *feel* anxious. I didn't discover that place. I also imagined I could write this book from the position of an expert. I've had to settle back into writing it as a student. I've been a student of anxiety most of my life. I'm seeking to be a student of peace now—inner peace, relational peace, and peace in the world about me.

But I write this book with a great sense of hope. My lifelong journey with anxiety has not been fruitless. I am learning how to live in the peaceful kingdom of Jesus. I'm learning that Paul just might be right when he suggests that I needn't worry (Philippians 4:6-7). Instead, I can learn how to regularly entrust my worries into the care of One who cares. I can live in a way where peace really does stand guard over my heart and mind. I'm learning that Peter just might be right that I can hand my worries over to Jesus because Jesus is interested in them and is Lord over them (1 Peter 5:7).

Whatever I have to say of value about anxiety in this book will be most helpful if it is spoken from actual weakness rather than presumed strength. We need to hear messages of lived mercy and grace. Talking about unlived theories doesn't help much.

So, a non-anxious life is about a certain pace of soul, pace of interaction, pace of engagement. Living a non-anxious life is about learning the pace of the kingdom, and God's kingdom has a particular pace. It's slower in all the best ways. It is an unhurried pace. It's admittedly a definition in the negative—God's kingdom is not in a hurry. But I've tried to offer *unhurried* as a virtuous, positive word for our purposes. Perhaps *non-anxious* can do the same work.

Peace is rooted in the robust and full-orbed meaning of the Hebrew *shalom*. It is more than an absence of tension, stress, conflict, or trouble. It is the presence of the Prince of Peace, the God of peace, the Spirit of peace. Peace is the atmosphere of heaven. And heaven surrounds and permeates us with peace we can breathe.

In the pages ahead, we'll see how Jesus can be our wise guide into the way of peace. We'll learn about good friends of peace like grace, hope, joy, and humility. We'll learn how to practice the presence of the Prince of Peace together.

Jesus embodies peace and gives to us as the world can never do. It is the peace of presence, not the peace of absence. Therefore, it is a peace that can guard our hearts and minds amid anxious feelings, anxious circumstances, anxious relationships. It is a peace we bring to our lived reality rather than a peace that we do not yet have and must seek elsewhere. Let's explore this non-anxious way of life together.

NON-ANXIOUS REFLECTION

You will find questions at the end of each chapter to use in reflection and journaling. You may want to discuss them with a spiritual friend or small group as well.

- How have you experienced God's peace in challenging situations that didn't resolve? What did that feel like? How did it compare to the peace of welcome circumstances or lack of trouble?

- Was there one of the anxiety metaphors that felt especially descriptive of your own experience (an operating system, a not-so-wonderful counselor, an anxious squirrel, a broken warning light, attempting time-travel, or a conspiracy theory)?

- What is currently tempting you to worry? What would it look like to translate that worrying into praying? How might you let anxious thoughts and feelings prompt you to pray rather than move you to worry? Ask for the help of God's Spirit in this.

2

ANXIETY ISN'T FOR THE BIRDS

The spiritual practice of silence has been important to my learning the ways of peace. Silence doesn't always quiet my anxious thoughts and feelings. Something in me wants to get noisy and busy again so I don't have to see how strong my anxiety is. Silence has often been more diagnostic than therapeutic for me.

So, in a particular moment of silence, sitting in my backyard on a sunny spring day, I was seeking to enjoy the presence of my Father in heaven. I felt the approach of familiar anxiety. But I also noticed the sound of birdsong surrounding me. One bird had a song that was a rapid-fire burst of chirps. She seemed nearly as insistent as my anxiety, but her message sounded something inviting, like, "I'm happy this morning. I'm well cared for. We have a Maker who watches over our lives. We are loved. It's why I sing this morning."

I heard the wisdom of Jesus in this. I heard Jesus inviting me to pay attention to the birds, as he invited a crowd to do on a hillside two thousand years ago (Matthew 6:25-27). The birds seemed to be reminding me that they do not go without. Without shopping or farming, they find a daily meal even in our backyard.

In the spirit of Jesus' birdwatching advice, I've taken to saying to myself, *Jesus just might be right about worry*. I'm not actually much in doubt about this idea. But my guts sometimes harbor a different sentiment than my cognitive confidence. Reminding my anxiety that Jesus might be right is my way of backing into truth. Jesus says that my noisy anxious thoughts and feelings do not have the last word.

The more I speak with leaders about hurry, the more I realize that a common form of soul hurry among us is anxiety. It's certainly true for me. My friend and bishop, Todd Hunter, once said in a sermon, "If it can be done in anxiety, it can be done better in peace." Doesn't that sound like kingdom wisdom? Doesn't it seem rather obviously true?

But, honestly, the first time I heard it, something in me rose up in strong resistance. Part of me disagreed with this word of wisdom; something in my gut questioned. I found myself wondering whether I'd get much done without my anxiety. I worried that I might not press myself to the same high standards that anxiety often pushed me to. I was strangely viewing my anxiety as an asset when Jesus was telling me that it was a liability.

BIRDS AS MENTORS

What does Jesus have to say about my worrying? How about his teaching on anxiety in his Sermon on the Mount? The idea about doing things better in peace drew me back to the original wisdom of Jesus, "Therefore I tell you, do not worry about your life" (Matthew 6:25).

How does Jesus want to help me overcome my habits of worry? He suggests a bit of birdwatching. "Look at the birds of the air; they do not sow or reap or store away in barns, and yet your heavenly Father feeds them. Are you not much more valuable than they?" (Matthew 6:26). Jesus wants us to notice that the birds don't appear to live in anxiety. They are not frantically worried about their next paycheck, or their next bill, let alone their next meal. Unlike us, they don't even do the work of sowing, reaping, and saving, and yet the Father cares for them.

I've taken Jesus' encouragement literally. Little by little, I've set up various birdfeeders in our backyard. There is a tray feeder with mixed seed that draws many different birds. There is a tube feeder with nyjer seed for the goldfinches and other small birds. There is a suet cake feeder that has drawn woodpeckers, scrub jays, crows, and even an occasional squirrel. Also, we keep a grape-jelly-and-sugar-water feeder for bright-yellow hooded orioles when they're up visiting from Central America.

I've enjoyed getting to know each bird's name and habits. They've become my friends. I've loved unexpected visitors, like the little pin-tailed whydah who decided the tray feeder was his personal domain. I find myself giving thanks for a family of scrub jays hanging around for a season. Over the last few years, I've noticed when some migrate in and back out.

Most of all, though, the birds have become my teachers in non-anxious living. I keep a downstairs office at home with a sliding glass door that looks out on all these feeders. At any moment, especially an anxious one, I can look out and see the birds enjoying what I've provided. And I can remember in that moment that what is provoking my anxiety is not outside the Father's provision for me. This reminder has been helping.

The care of God for his creation, such as the birds, is an expression of pure grace. God's provision is more like a gift than a paycheck. Grace precludes any orientation to earning, but my anxiety tends to be *rooted* in an earning perspective on my life and work. Do I or don't I deserve what God provides? The birds don't seem to be wrestling much with this. God isn't assessing whether I deserve what he gives moment to moment. God's nature is generous, and so God's interaction with me is rooted in grace.

God cares for the birds who aren't doing much to change the world. They are precious to God, but we, made in his image, are far more precious to the Father. If God graciously cares for little birds who are here today and gone tomorrow, how much more will God care for women and men made in his very image who will live forever? In light of this reality, anxiety is a less realistic response than confidence and peace is. This isn't a condemning correction. This is a simple, kind statement of kingdom reality. We have a Father who cares for us well and constantly.

My anxieties are a kind of soul amnesia. I forget that God is constantly caring and providing for me. Perhaps this is why God invites us to "remember" so often in Scripture. Remembering the care of God is a good practice for our souls.

A MISGUIDED EQUATION

I grew up assuming the truth of this equation: *anxiety equals love.* I believed that the only way I could prove that I really cared about someone or something was to frantically worry. But if you've ever been the one being frantically worried about, you know it doesn't feel much like you're the focus of the caring. When I frantically worry about another person, I don't think they actually feel care from me. I'm more likely putting pressure on them to do something that will make me worry less (as though my worry were mainly dependent on something they do or don't do).

Instead, I've come to believe in a better equation to describe what anxiety does: *anxiety equals care minus God.* We use the word *care* for both anxiety and love. We speak of not having a care in the world: that's about anxiety. We tell someone we care for them: that's love. The thing is, peace and love are very good friends. Anxiety and love have a hard time hanging out together.

Anxiety is concern that isn't rooted in the faithful presence of God. It has become detached from the love of God or has lost touch with its reality. Without faith I can't be at home in the pleasure of God. In anxiety, I can't either. Worry has a way of blinding me to the measureless faithfulness of Christ, who is Immanuel—God-with-me. God-with-me is my greatest protection from anxious fretting. Worry focuses on my shortcomings or challenges and doesn't notice the far greater realities of God's goodness, power, and love with me.

Care does good things for the beloved. Anxiety doesn't. It is a negation rather than a positive action. I find that I'm more able to love others when I'm rooted in the soil of trust, confidence, and knowing myself loved by God. I then care for others from abundance. My worry doesn't give good things to the ones I'm worrying about.

This is what praying our anxieties helps us remember. We can root our anxious concerns into the love of God. We can offer our worrisome cares into the care of our Father. This can transform them from fruitless worries to fruitful love. I can redeem the passion and energy of my worries.

My anxiety often feels like an echo chamber of my own thoughts that becomes noisier over time. When I allow God's Spirit to draw my attention away from my own concerns to notice and engage the concerns of others, my anxiety often quiets. When I think about others, pray for others, reach out to others, care for others, I am less overwhelmed by my own anxious thoughts. My attention is drawn away from the centrifugal force of my own worry. Love displaces both fear and worry.

I CALL YOU FRIENDS

Jesus speaks about his and the Father's love for us in his words to his inner circle in the upper room. "You are my friends if you do what I command. I no longer call you servants, because a servant does not know his master's business. Instead, I have called you friends, for everything that I learned from my Father I have made known to you" (John 15:14-15). What inviting words Jesus speaks.

I've found that my inner vision of Jesus impacts my anxiety levels. How do I assume Jesus is relating to me: as a servant, or as a friend? When I think of myself first as servant—mostly as someone who does things *for* Jesus—I tend to measure myself by what I am (or am not) accomplishing in my service. But Jesus tells his inner circle that he doesn't think of them (or us) first as servants, but as friends.

Jesus tells them that servants are not in on the master's business. They serve the master's purpose but are not included in the master's counsels. They get assignments. They are given orders. But friends? They enjoy conversation, hear the master's heart, and learn the master's purposes.

Jesus wants us to experience his Father's table, not just serve at it. Servants visit the table. Friends sit at the table. Servants serve at a distance. Friends are invited to linger in the master's presence. Such loving friendship with the Father and the Son is a place of peace. It is in this way that we best honor the Father—not first with our service *for* God but through our cooperative friendship *with* God.

So, I come first as a friend listening for Jesus who wishes to walk together rather than first as a servant who is working for him at a distance. Growing in this friendship has borne in me the fruit of confidence, authority, and fruitfulness. It is living and growing in this friendship with God in Christ that causes our lives to be like the good branch that bears much quality fruit.

Later in his teachings to the inner circle, Jesus again affirms that the Father loves them in the same way that they have come to experience the affectionate friendship of Jesus. "No, the Father himself loves you because you have loved me and have believed that I came from God" (John 16:27). When my soul is aware of the reality of the Father's love for me, it's hard for anxiety to remain strong. Jesus wants us to trust that the Father's posture toward us is as loving as his. Love really does cast out fear and displace anxiety.

There lingers in me the gut image of a God that is unpleasable, harsh, or demanding instead of loving. So much of my recent journey with Jesus has been about cultivating the habit of becoming at home in the loving presence of God. Trusting in the reality of God's love creates an atmosphere that has weakened the potency of anxiety in my life.

I've realized that trusting in the love of God in Christ can be an overarching reality even in the presence of strong and unpleasant emotion (like my anxiety). I don't have to avoid or hide from anxiety. I can acknowledge its presence amid the greater presence of God's love. At home in God's love, I thrive and anxiety doesn't.

YOU DON'T HAVE TO WORRY

As Jesus continues his teaching in Matthew 6, he goes on to give us a very good reason to let go of our worrying habits by asking a very simple question: "Can any one of you by worrying add a single hour to your life?" (Matthew 6:27). Worrying doesn't extend my life even an hour; it might even shorten it. Worrying doesn't make me one inch taller; it just might make me shorter as I stoop under the burden of my worries.

When Jesus tells us, "Don't worry about your life," I don't primarily hear him saying, "You *shouldn't* worry!" That sort of *should* has a way of making me worry *more* about my worrying. That doesn't help. Instead, I believe the spirit of Jesus' gracious counsel is more like, "You don't *have* to worry."

Worry doesn't help. It doesn't improve anything. My worry is rooted in an unfortunate experiential blindness to the reality of God's presence and God's care in my present situation. But Jesus says worry does nothing to improve my life or my situation. As I've said, Jesus is speaking to my strange assumption that anxiety is somehow an asset to me. I assumed that it was anxiety that best got me going and kept me doing good work. Anxiety kept me busy, which I assumed was good. Anxiety, combined with perfectionism, drove me to high standards and big achievements. What could be wrong with that?

Anxiety might get me moving and get things done, but if anxiety is fuel, it's fuel that burns dirty. It has a way of fouling my health, my relationships, and the actual quality of my work. Peace, on the other hand, gives me access to the green energy of fellowship with God's Spirit. It burns clean with joy and hope. Anxiety presses me into tunnel vision, when peace would give me a grander perspective and a relaxed approach to my next step. Anxiety drives me into some frantic next thing, when instead I might be able to see many good options before me. Anxiety has a way of keeping me busy with things that don't matter, whereas peace keeps me in a place where I see with perspective what *really* matters.

So, again, Jesus just might be right about my anxieties. When my anxiety claims to provide me reliable information about my immediate future, it's been wrong far more often than it's been right. Anxiety is a miserably poor predictor of my actual future. You could call it a false prophet and you wouldn't be wrong. As Mark Twain put it, "I've had a lot of worries in my life, most of which never happened." Yet I still often assume that my feeling of anxiety is a reliable indicator that something terrible is going to happen soon.

NOTICE THE FLOWERS

To birdwatching, Jesus adds his recommendation that we notice the beauty of the flowers. "And why do you worry about clothes? See how the flowers of the field grow. They do not labor or spin. Yet I tell you that not even Solomon in all his splendor was dressed like one of these" (Matthew 6:28-29). God *gives* the flowers a beauty that we can't match with our best creative efforts. Flowers don't make themselves beautiful. They are the creative expression of the Divine Artist.

Flowers aren't anxiously attempting to be more beautiful. They aren't investing immense energy in managing their appearance to other flowers. God has *given* them beauty. And the beauty of our own lives is not primarily a thing we achieve, but something we are given. What makes our lives winsome and attractive is given to us; it's not self-created. It is more rooted in who we are than in how we look. The majesty of our lives is established and shines from our divinely created being.

The beauty of flowers is measured in days or perhaps weeks. "If that is how God clothes the grass of the field, which is here today and tomorrow is thrown into the fire, will he not much more clothe you—you of little faith?" (Matthew 6:30). Jesus is letting us know that the beauty of our lives is of a lasting sort. Flowers come and go. We enjoy having cut flowers in our home. We also enjoy keeping around live plants that bloom. Over decades, we've had hundreds of flowering plants that have come and gone. But the beauty with which God clothes us—you and me—is intended for eternity. It is greater than the beauty of youth that also comes and goes. The beauty of a soul reflecting the glory of its Maker is the beauty that lasts.

We live in a culture that is captured by the cuteness of youth. We spend immense amounts of time, money, and effort attempting to hold onto youth for as long as we can. But time always diminishes, little by little, the glory of youth. True beauty runs much deeper than this. Jesus points to its source—faith. Worry and anxiety are opposed to simple trust; they do not add anything to the beauty of our lives. And simple trust is the mirror by which we reflect the faithful, gracious, glorious beauty of God in Christ.

WHAT IF?

So, in the light of our attention to God's care for the birds and his beautification of the flowers, Jesus reminds us again that he's talking to us about our anxiety. "So do not worry, saying, 'What shall we eat?' or 'What shall we drink?' or 'What shall we wear?' For the pagans run after all these things, and your heavenly Father knows that you need them" (Matthew 6:31-32). All of these worry questions begin with the words "What shall we?" Many of my most worrisome thoughts begin with similar words: "What if?"

My what ifs are rarely about food and clothing. I know that these are the worries of so many in our world and my heart breaks. God cares especially for those who are poor, and invites us to extend his care to these sisters and brothers ourselves. It would help us remember that our many "first world problems" are not nearly as life-threatening as we imagine. Being confronted by the degree of basic human need around the world has graciously changed my perspective on my own usual worries.

In his teaching, Jesus suggests that those with no trusting vision of God in their lives (he calls them "pagans") spend a lot of time chasing after the things they need or think they need. They have no sense that the good things they need in their lives are gifts from their Maker, that their lives consist of far more than acquiring stuff. It is God's generosity that makes our lives beautiful. When I spend a lot of time worrying about what I want and need, I'm little different from these "pagans." I'm a functional atheist.

Such behavior reflects little sense of a trusting connection with a Father in heaven who knows us, cares for us, provides for us. The Father of Jesus is our Father. Such a good Father knows just what we need. I've sometimes spent time worrying about something God is trying to prepare me to receive. The grace of God is the way God relates and interacts with us. God is not a heavenly dispensary. God is a loving Father, ever-present to treat us with care and generosity. As I grow to trust this as my reality, my anxieties and worries have a way of burning off like a morning mist.

This is where Jesus sums up his counsel with familiar words: "But seek first his kingdom and his righteousness, and all these things will be given to you as well" (Matthew 6:33). My frantic worry is a different sort of "seek first." I've sometimes trained myself to turn first to worry rather than learning to turn first to my gracious God-with-me. This sort of seeking has a way of draining my life of beauty, buoyancy, and abundance. But I find these when I gaze on God in trust. God really is reigning in our world today, despite much apparent evidence to the contrary.

God really knows what he's doing. I'm learning to orient my attention toward God's kingdom and righteousness.

As Jesus sums up his training about anxiety, he touches a theme that is common to many of our worries. While some of our worries are about how something went or how something is going now, many of our worries point to an uncertain future. So Jesus says, "Therefore do not worry about tomorrow, for tomorrow will worry about itself. Each day has enough trouble of its own" (Matthew 6:34). The uncertainty of our future is met with the certainty of who God is, now and in the future—the same yesterday, today, and forever.

When I worry about tomorrow, I am attempting to import future concerns into today. I imagine the concerns of each day as though they were a series of blocks stretching out into the future. One block of concerns for one day is manageable (and often still challenging). But my anxiety has a habit of gathering future blocks and piling them all onto today. This becomes overwhelming. Instead of a future that looks like manageable daily concerns stretching before me, I see day after day piled high with more worries than I can bear.

I've sometimes been in the habit of carrying *every* upcoming task or project as a present burden. I have talk notes to prepare, a book project to continue, notes for an upcoming sermon, people to meet with, and I behave as though I must complete all these *right* now. As I write that sentence, I realize how silly it sounds, but my emotions too often buy it completely. I'm like an octopus trying to hold onto every piece of upcoming work right now. It's not surprising that I feel overwhelmed.

Managing the concerns of tomorrow (or the next day or the next) is not even possible. I'm not there yet. God may be, but I'm not. I have only today. I have only this moment. Of course I make plans for the future, but even those are not set in cement. I make my plans, but I am often surprised when I get to the point in time I'd envisioned. I have only the present moment to live and to do whatever lies before me. Peace is with me in that present.

When I envision focusing on just one of these tasks or projects, I feel some relief. Energy arises. I feel more hopeful and less burdened. And I remember that Immanuel, the God of grace and peace, is here with me.

NON-ANXIOUS REFLECTION

- The chapter opens with an invitation to the practice of silence. Why not experiment with five minutes of quiet now? When you're quiet, what arises in your thoughts and emotions? See if you can simply notice what arises rather than letting yourself be overwhelmed by it. Offer yourself to the God of peace with you in the presence of these thoughts and emotions.

- Why not experiment with a little birdwatching in the spirit of Jesus' teaching? When you look out the window or step outside, do you see or hear any birds around? What do you notice? What wisdom might God's Spirit be giving as you look, listen, and pray?

- Is there a "What if?" that has been pestering your heart and mind? Why not experiment with offering that worry to the God who is with you now and who is well aware of your actual future? See if you can't enter into a sense of God's care for you in this moment and in the moments to come.

3

STUDENTS BECOME MENTORS

In my journey to become more a student of peace and less a student of anxiety, I have not arrived. I am not perfect. But I am grateful for progress. I'm glad that anxiety is less often an autopilot mode for me now. Progress is what we all are aiming at in our life with God. Perfectionism has been paralyzing for me; celebrating spiritual progress has been freeing and life-giving. When we are making progress in our life in Christ, we can share with others the wisdom of what we're learning. We can find courage to echo the heart of Paul the apostle when he says, "Follow my example, just like I follow Christ's" (1 Corinthians 11:1 CEB). That's what I'm doing in these pages.

THE APOSTLE PAUL'S COUNSEL

Paul understood what Jesus was saying about anxiety. He says, "Don't fret or worry. Instead of worrying, pray. Let petitions and praises shape your worries into prayers, letting God know your concerns. Before you know it, a sense of God's wholeness, everything coming together for good, will come and settle you down. It's wonderful what happens when Christ displaces worry at the center of your life" (Philippians 4:6-7 MSG).

I've learned that when I *feel* worry, I can still choose peace. I can engage God in prayerful listening and conversation. I can talk with God and others about what concerns me. I can ask God for what I feel I need. I can express praise and gratitude for God who is not erratic like me. I can pray my concerns instead of worrying them. And I can learn how to hand my concerns over to God's care.

One of the challenges for me is learning how not to worry about my worries. I find myself feeling anxious, and then I add thoughts of worry to my feelings of worry. I worry about my worries, and then I worry that I'm worrying about my worries. I interpret my feelings of anxiety as ultimate reality. But, if I stay at my practice, I discover that there really is a peace and well-being that reflects the reality of God's wholeness and his reliable presence with me, settling and quieting my heart and mind. I am not alone, and the One who is with me is good, caring, and capable. It really is wonderful what happens when the Prince of Peace displaces worry at the center of my life.

My anxious worry isn't so much breaking a rule as it is making a mistake about reality. Whatever I imagine may do me irreparable harm in the future lies within the caring and powerful hands of my Father in heaven. Bad things have happened to me; worse things have happened to some who are dear to me. I still believe that anxious worry hasn't improved anyone's circumstances.

Paul invites me to a situational response. Something arises that provokes my anxieties: I discover a mistake I've made; some element of my plan gets upended by an interruption; something is asked of me that stretches my sense of competency and capability. For me, these are often unpleasant surprises and I feel anxious.

RESPONDING TO ANXIETY

In those moments when the red light of anxiety flashes on my dashboard, I'm learning to remember that it may be an indicator of something out of alignment rather than assuming it is a sign of something actually bad. Paul's strategy is simple—replace the ruminating and the mulling with a response rooted in four words: prayer, petition, thanksgiving, request. These aren't exactly four distinct movements, but together they offer a better approach than worrying about that which provokes anxiety.

Prayer. Talk with God about your concerns rather than talking with yourself about them. My worrying ends up a self-focused activity. Even if I worry about other people or situations, I'm usually doing it in the tight confines of my own thoughts, feelings, and sensations. Worry tends to turn me in on myself. This might be why it feels so constricting and compressing. I can cultivate the habit of responding to emotional, cognitive, and even physical indicators of anxiety by turning toward God.

What might such a prayer sound like? "Lord, I'm feeling anxious again. There is that familiar tightness in my chest and the spinning thoughts. There is the sinking feeling of dread in my gut. But I am not alone. You are with me, and you are greater than what overwhelms me, real or imagined. Enable me to have your perspective in this moment. Open my eyes wider than this red light on the dashboard of my awareness."

Petition. A petition is bringing our situation before God, who cares and is capable to act on our behalf. We ask God to do for us what we are powerless to do for ourselves. In an odd way, my anxiety is often an attempt to be a god to myself. I'm attempting sovereignty. I'm working to wrap my arms around what worries me. But my arms are much smaller than I think in terms of how much they can hold and control.

So I bring my petition before the only Sovereign there actually is. I acknowledge that this God is for me and is working for my good. God's work is much more effective than the way circumstances affect me.

Thanksgiving. Gratitude has proven to be a very powerful antidote to my habit of worry. Gratitude is acknowledging that the reality of God's grace is larger than the reality (or even the perceived reality) of a threat I anticipate. Rather than my life being mostly full of bad things to fear, it is actually full of so many good things to celebrate.

Paul writes about worry from a Roman prison. It's not a nice place to be stuck month after month. But this is where he shares his strategy about anxiety. This is the secret he has learned about the soul-sucking practice of worry.

How do we grow in gratitude for the good that is already present in our lives? How do we find freedom from the anxious morality of measuring our spiritual practices, and enter into the richness of being in God's good grace? How do we become rooted in a contentment that is strong, whether in plenty or in want? A few lines from the Psalms help me immensely here.

Gratitude helps me enter into a flourishing life that is far better than an anxious life. The psalmist says this about flourishing: "The righteous will flourish like a palm tree, they will grow like a cedar of Lebanon; planted in the house of the LORD, they will flourish in the courts of our God. They will still bear fruit in old age, they will stay fresh and green, proclaiming, 'The LORD is upright; he is my Rock, and there is no wickedness in him'" (Psalm 92:12-15).

Flourishing like a palm tree says that I can flourish just about anywhere. I've seen palm trees flourishing in the nearby desert of Palm Springs. I've seen palm trees flourishing in the lushness of the Dominican Republic and Hawaii. Palm trees flourish in locations of plenty and in locations of want. I want to be fresh and green even into my elder years. I learn to flourish like this in the presence of God—practicing gratitude, embracing the gift of righteousness rather than trying to measure out my own, deepening roots of contentment in the presence of God.

Requests. What do you wish to ask God for? What would help you right now? Ask and watch for God's wise, loving response. Let this be the focus of your attention. Let this be your meditation rather than imagining catastrophic futures that may never be realized. Direct the energy of anxiety into the activity of prayer. My anxiety has been so often wrong about the future anyway. Hasn't yours?

When we come to God in these prayerful ways, Paul says that God's peace will protect our hearts and minds from corrosive worries in a way that is beyond comprehending. It's not that this peace doesn't make sense, but that it only makes sense in view of the powerful presence of God-with-us. It isn't a peace explained by the removal of troubles or the absence of difficulties. It is a peace that transcends understanding because it is the peace of God who is bigger than our understanding.

PRAYING OR REHEARSING OUR WORRIES

I'm learning that I can offer my worries to God and let God hold onto them instead of me. Rather than rehearsing my worries in the presence of God, then taking them back to chew on, I can learn to stop ruminating on my worries—to cease worrying about my worries and being anxious about my anxieties. Sometimes I imagine that my worries are like anxious little children. I answer their young and worrisome "what ifs" with compassion, empathy, care, and presence, and that helps me find peace.

There is a way of bringing my anxieties to God with an intention to release them into his hands and welcome the gift of his guarding peace. There is also a way of rehearsing my anxieties in God's presence so that I leave with them still in my clinging hands. I mull my worries in God's presence rather than releasing them. I can pray *in* my anxieties, or pray my way *out of* them. I can learn to see my worries with a bit of holy distance rather than simply being trapped in the middle of them.

We can learn to translate our anxieties into prayers. We can redirect the energy of worry into the activity of prayer. What I've come to believe is that my worries are God-given energies misdirected. Rather than try to get rid of worries, it helps me to direct their energy toward God to ask God for what I fear I lack (or will lack in some future moment). My worry is misguided concern. It is a strange sort of love turned upside down; my worries are evidence of care. I won't pray long for someone (or something) I don't care about. Bringing that soul concern before God is acknowledging that God cares more than I do, is more capable and wise than I am, and is already at work in ways I'll never be able to be. There is a way to bring worries to God and take God's peace with me as I go on my way.

The desert fathers remind us that anxiety is the death of prayer.[1] But true prayer—vital communion with the living God—is also the death of anxiety.

THINKING PEACE

Following Paul's counsel about how to navigate anxiety through prayer, he then speaks to us about our thoughts. It has taken me a while to learn that I don't have to add anxious thoughts to my anxious feelings. I've found a lot of wisdom in Paul's words, "Finally, brothers and sisters, whatever is true, whatever is noble, whatever is right, whatever is pure, whatever is lovely, whatever is admirable—if anything is excellent or praiseworthy—think about such things. Whatever you have learned or received or heard from me, or seen in me—put it into practice. And the God of peace will be with you" (Philippians 4:8-9).

"And the God of peace will be with you" is not a recompense for good thinking patterns. Paul lays out a way of thinking and living that keeps us alert to the presence of the God of peace who is always with us. There is a way to live rich in the kingdom that is worth talking about. Paul describes this way of abiding with the God of peace in a series of inviting words.

True. There is peace when we live in keeping with reality. Even when reality is hard or painful, we are in a better place living in truth rather than denying it or pretending about it. There is so much that is good in the reality of God's kingdom.

Noble. Peace flourishes in an honest, reverent soul. The peace of God is a royal way to life.

Right. The Psalms tell us that "righteousness and peace kiss each other" (Psalm 85:10). Peace does good to others. Peace gives God and people their due. Anxiety really doesn't.

Pure. Purity is when something is what it was meant to be. For example, we prefer our milk to be "holy." When you open a carton of milk, you don't want to see blades of grass or flecks of dirt floating around on top. What you want is milk, only milk, pure milk. This sort of divine simplicity is good friends with peace of heart and of relationship.

Lovely. Peace is attractive. It's beautiful. Anxiety isn't. I want to live a life that others find inviting.

Admirable. When we fill our minds with that which inspires us, with things of good reputation, we will find ourselves more relaxed inside and less likely to offend others.

When this is our way of thinking, we will find peace of mind and heart, and peace in our relationships far deeper and more secure. This is where we focus our attention so that peace is a natural fruit. All of this is what it looks like for the peace of God to stand guard over our hearts and minds. These ways of thinking and living root us more deeply in the God of peace who is always with us.

We find growing freedom from worry as we live in conversational relationship with the God of peace, when we learn to fill our minds with the beautiful reality of God's kingdom, and by letting our lives be increasingly shaped by God's counsel and teaching about the way of peace.

TRANSFERRING OUR CARES TO GOD

Like Paul, Peter had learned the ways of the Prince of Peace. As his student, Peter was present that day when Jesus taught the crowds about anxiety. Peter took the counsel of Jesus to heart so well that he later became a teacher to others. Listen to words from his first letter about what he had learned about anxiety: "Humble yourselves, therefore, under the mighty hand of God so that at the proper time he may exalt you, casting all your anxieties on him, because he cares for you" (1 Peter 5:6-7 ESV). How remarkable that Peter, who had such a tendency for over-confidence and self-assurance in his youth, roots his vision of a non-anxious life in the context of humility.

In my experience, humility and peace are good friends. Pride and anxiety are unfortunately close companions as well. But when I talk about pride here, I want to be clear. Pride is not just about a self-promoting, self-important, boastful orientation to life. That is a common variety of pride to be sure. But pride, more simply, is a kind of self-focusing attempt to live self-contained. Pride is an orientation to life with little to no confidence in the practical good of God's presence in my life. That's the way in which I've seen anxiety and pride relate.

When I try to take responsibility for what is God's to care for, I find myself anxious. This sort of anxiety is a symptom of my mistaken attempt at personal sovereignty. I imagine that I can control situations and people to protect myself from potential harm. It doesn't feel like pride in the moment, but that's what it ends up being. My pride says, "If I don't take care of myself, who else will?" Humility invites me to say instead, "I am free to live well because God cares well for me." Humility is healthy alignment with kingdom reality; pride is anxious misalignment.

When I've come to humbly trust God's powerful care, I recognize that I am in God's gracious protection and care. God does not necessarily keep bad things from happening in my life. We all know this from experience. But God is not overwhelmed by the bad things that happen to us, and is able to help us navigate these things with humble courage. This is how the way of humility has proven to be a way of peace for me.

THE GIFT OF REPETITION

I was once leading a multiday retreat for the leadership team of a very large church. There were about seventy-five staff members in the room. I had already made a plan for the curriculum of the retreat, but woke one morning with what felt like a divine nudge to do something I *hadn't* planned.

My heart was drawn to Psalm 136 as an opening exercise for the morning. The second line of all twenty-seven verses is "His love endures forever." It's a beautiful, biblical example of meaningful repetition. In the flow of the psalm, those first lines begin in thanksgiving, move to affirming God as creator, deliverer, guide, provider, and then turn to thanksgiving in closing.

Many of our churches don't include much experience with repetition like this. We might even feel a bit anxious with such a monotonous practice in our church service. We often have a bias toward doing something new all the time. So I was a bit nervous with what I felt nudged to do with this leadership team. When we gathered that morning, the first thing we did together was engage this psalm antiphonally. I explained that I was going to read the first line of each verse, and then I would invite them to respond as a community with "His love endures forever." About five or six verses into the exercise, I sensed at least a few in the room were beginning to feel uncomfortable with unfamiliar repetition. And we still had twenty verses to go.

As the exercise continued, the group began to visibly settle into their four-word response. The reality of God's enduring love for them was sinking in. When we had walked our way through the psalm together in this way, I suggested that there may well be sentences we would like to speak aloud in recognition of our own experience of God's person, God as creator, deliverer, or provider, or in thanks to God. I invited them to call out sentences like that in the midst of our gathering and said that we all would respond again with those four words. There were probably about twenty more sentences of praise or thanksgiving to which we responded with "His love endures forever."

My own experience of anxiety has often been repetitious in nature. I find my thoughts looping through rehearsing things that I wish had happened differently (or how I wish I'd responded differently). Or I find myself anticipating some potential future problem or crisis and try to work out how to resolve or mitigate its impact. A practice like engaging Psalm 136 as we did enables me to engage a holy repetition that combats the unholy repetition my anxiety drives. This holy practice of repetition can help me grow as a student of the Prince of Peace.

NON-ANXIOUS REFLECTION

- What might it feel like for the presence of Christ to displace worry at the center of your life? Are you currently aware of anxiety in your thoughts or emotions? Why not ask Jesus to help you sense the reality of his presence in you by the Spirit and see if his peace might begin to displace anxiety? Be patient with this practice.

- Take a moment to review the four prayer words Paul uses in Philippians 4:6-7 to counsel us in dealing with our anxieties: prayer, petition, thanksgiving, request. Is there one that seems especially important or inviting to you? Why not take a moment to practice it in God's presence now?

- Do you identify with the difference between ruminating your worries and praying your worries? If so, in what way? Reflect on whether you may be focusing on your worries in the presence of God, or focusing on God in the midst of your worries. Interact with God about this.

- We unpacked a way of thinking that Paul recommends, in which we find ourselves at home in the presence of the God of peace. Is there one of those qualities of thought that feels especially timely for you today (true, noble, right, pure, lovely, admirable, excellent, praiseworthy)? How is God with you in these ways today?

4

GRACIOUS FULLNESS

As an Anglican priest, I am guided in my morning prayers by the Book of Common Prayer. The very first line in the liturgy for morning prayer is, simply, "Grace to you and peace from God our Father and the Lord Jesus Christ." In these words, I remember who God is. I remember who I am. And I begin my day in the generous and restful presence of God.

A mentor of mine, Wayne Anderson, once spent months reviewing and reflecting on the language of *grace* throughout the Scriptures.[1] When he came to Paul's letters, he noticed that each mentioned the grace of God in the opening lines. He also noticed that the very last word of the Christian Scriptures is a blessing of grace: "The grace of the Lord Jesus be with God's people. Amen" (Revelation 22:21). The Scriptures begin with a gracious creation, "Let there be light" (Genesis 1:3). From beginning to end, we are living in a story of God's generous grace.

Wayne was once sharing these insights with a group of pastors when he noticed one pastor furiously thumbing through the pages of his Bible. Wayne wondered if perhaps this pastor didn't believe his comment about grace opening every letter of Paul's. After his presentation, the pastor came up to talk, intent and serious looking. He said, "You know how you said that every single letter of Paul's begins with grace?" Wayne braced himself for some correction or mitigation of his confident statement. "Well, did you know that every single letter of Paul's *ends* with grace as well?"[2] Grace is the origin and the culmination of the gospel Paul preached.

There is another word that begins every letter Paul writes to a church: *peace*. Sometimes he greets them as simply as, "Grace and peace to you" (1 Thessalonians 1:1). Most often, his warmhearted greeting is "Grace and peace to you from God our Father and from the Lord Jesus Christ."[3] Grace and peace are longtime friends. They are at home with each other.

God's grace reminds me that I'm never alone. Anxiety seeks to convince me that I have only myself to count on. Grace reminds me that God is very much for me. Anxiety tries to persuade me that everything is against me. But I don't *achieve* my life, I *receive* my life day by day. Grace reminds me that the reality of my life is to welcome it with gratitude. Anxiety expects me to earn what I need, or to deserve what would bless me.

Paul's opening (and sometimes closing) of his letters with "grace and peace" is more than a shallow convention. It represents his core vision of our life together in the kingdom. We all live by God's grace and we live in God's peace. What would a grace-and-peace-rooted identity look like? How do grace-and-peace-guided relationships work? How does grace-empowered work engaged in peace operate? How might grace become the fuel and peace become the context for our Christian witness?

So in all his letters, Paul begins with the blessing of God's grace and peace. There have been times when I'm tempted to move past what has felt to me to be appropriate but mostly unimportant opening words in Paul's letters. He has to say *something* before he gets down to business. Over time, however, I've come to experience those little words as substantial and foundational.

INHALING GRACE

What does it look like to *live* grace and peace? I find that deep peace is rooted in the growing confidence that my life really is *graced*. The grace of God is the atmosphere of God's kingdom. We live by inhaling grace. We weren't made to breath anxiety, fear, or insecurity. When we try to inhale these, we find they choke us rather than sustain us.

What does it look like when the grace of God bears the fruit of peace in our lives, our relationships, even our work? God's generosity enables us to resist the temptation to presume our lives are meager rather than abundant. God's gracious initiative buoys me and carries me along in this good kingdom way of living and serving. God's empowering presence gives me humble courage to bless others, knowing that I give from a limitless source of goodness available to me in God. God's affection and delight in me free me from craving the recognition of others, which frees me to live for their good more than for my own. God's merciful forgiveness releases me from the burden of shame and guilt that has sometimes driven me to unhealthy ways of relating to others.

My soul breathes grace. God the Father and the Lord Jesus simply *are* gracious. When I've entertained gut images of God that are less than gracious—judgmental, impatient, harsh, or unkind—it isn't surprising that my life isn't very peaceful. I find myself trying to earn favor from that judgmental God. I find myself tiptoeing around an impatient God. I try to be extra nice around a harsh and unkind God. There isn't much peace in such a posture.

My wife, Gem, and I were once on what we call a "walk and talk," and she was sharing how God had been bringing to mind past grace as a place of current reflection and enjoyment. Gem is better at this than I am. The practice was God's Spirit recalling to Gem's heart recent meaningful moments on which she could reflect and from which she could draw life and encouragement. I tend to always look for something new and forget how much good I've already received from and enjoyed in God.

Notice how often God reminds Israel of their exodus story with him. It's as though that grace in their history was so rich that they hadn't begun to fully mine its goodness. It's beautiful when we recall moments of great goodness in our own history and relish that grace. It is as much ours today as it was then.

Going back to Paul's "grace and peace" blessing to the churches, he adds a third word in his letter to his young friend and fellow worker, Timothy. He says, "Grace, *mercy* and peace to you" (1 Timothy 1:2; 2 Timothy 1:2, emphasis added). The longer I've lived as a Christian, the more I have recognized my deep need for mercy. Maturity includes a growing awareness of our need of both mercy and grace. When someone lives as a Christian under the belief that their need for mercy diminishes over time, that's not a reflection of reality.

This is the trajectory of self-righteousness rather than kingdom-first righteousness. It is the direction of judgmentalism rather than love. It is the wide path of presumption rather than the narrow path of true growth. We fail to extend mercy to others when our own felt need for mercy diminishes. But living in the generous grace and the lavish mercy of God bears the fruit of deep peace in our lives.

GRACE AND PRAYER

In practice, one of the ways we learn to live in the grace of God is through prayer. By this, I don't mean speaking a lot of words at

God. I mean learning to live in conversational relationship with God, moment by moment.

When I read Paul's prayers in his letters, I like to imagine what Paul expected his prayers to become in the lives of those for whom he prayed. What particular grace did he anticipate they would gain as he prayed for them? A beautiful example of prayer cooperating with grace is Paul's prayer for his friends in Ephesus.

> I pray that out of his glorious riches he may strengthen you with power through his Spirit in your inner being, so that Christ may dwell in your hearts through faith. And I pray that you, being rooted and established in love, may have power, together with all the Lord's holy people, to grasp how wide and long and high and deep is the love of Christ, and to know this love that surpasses knowledge—that you may be filled to the measure of all the fullness of God. (Ephesians 3:16-19)

This prayer is rooted in grace. Paul envisioned something good that would come to his friends out of God's "glorious riches." Paul expected that his prayer answered would look like people experiencing Christ more and more at home in their hearts. He anticipated that they would be more deeply rooted in relationship with Christ. He assumed that they would be more able to grasp the measureless immensity of Christ's love. He expected that they would be more and more full of all God's fullness. While the language of peace is not present, the fruit of peace is.

When we pray for others, we are drawing on the ever-present grace of God for their good. We are bringing others into the presence of God-with-us. We are inviting God's rich grace to encourage, to guide, and to make fruitful the lives of those we care about.

GRACE AND THIRST

Anxiety is often about making sure that my thirsts are met. What sort of thirsts? Sometimes I feel unsafe, and I'm seeking the perceived protection of trying to accurately predict or control the future. Sometimes I feel in disarray and I'm seeking to frantically organize my life in a way that makes sense to me. Sometimes I feel hungry for words of affirmation and I'm restlessly seeking to impress those around me. Sometimes I feel inadequate and I'm anxiously seeking to feel a bit more confident or in control of my life. But the strategies of anxiety, for all its fretting, don't manage to meet these needs.

Though my soul seeks rest in all these ways, there is only one way in which my soul finds rest. In communion with God, my life always gains security, order, affirmation, and confidence. Maybe that sounds like pious religious language to some ears. But I have proven its truth in both my embrace of it and my resistance to it.

Anxiety may be an attempt at survival, but peace is an atmosphere in which we can actually thrive. Anxiety worries that there won't be enough for me. It assumes that life is a zero-sum game. Someone else's gain is automatically my loss. Someone else's success guarantees a catastrophe for me. But the peaceable kingdom of God is under no such limits. It is the realm of limitless abundance because it is ruled by an eternal and infinitely good King. When I've come to trust this as my daily reality, I've found that, in my anxiety, I am grasping for something I already have. I am seeking something I've already been given.

Worrying in the presence of such a gracious God is like going hungry while seated at a lavish table full of fine food. Anxiety here is like a blindfold and nose plugs. I find that I can't perceive God's delicious provision at such an extravagant table. Anxiety makes us blind to the great goodness God is always providing. Anxiety makes us deaf to the gracious words of God that the Spirit is speaking. Anxiety dulls our sense of smell for the sweetness and richness of God's delightful gifts. Worry fails to discern and trust in God's real, present, and abundant grace.

GOD LONGS TO BE GRACIOUS

Another of my favorite descriptions of God and his grace is Isaiah's, "The LORD longs to be gracious to you, therefore he will rise up to show you compassion" (Isaiah 30:18). Anxiety will find it quite difficult to linger in the presence of such remarkable goodness. Grace reminds me that I have more than I need. Anxiety complains that there will never be enough.

God does not reluctantly consent to show us grace. God is not begrudging in his generosity. God's grace does not come in wisps or trickles. It is a roaring river of generous presence. It is the deep desire of God's heart to entrust us with immeasurable love and compassion. What a gift when my vision of God is being shaped and transformed by this generous picture. I can learn to open more fully to such grace and compassion. I can resist the ways that fear, worry, or distraction would hinder me from receiving and embracing the generosity of God.

Too often, a vision of my shortcomings has filled my awareness more than a vision of God's love for generosity, mercy, and grace. The prophet Isaiah later offers that "[the LORD] will be the sure foundation for your times, a rich store of salvation and wisdom and knowledge; the fear of the LORD is the key to this treasure" (Isaiah 33:6). When my worries tell me that my life is nothing but shaky, that I'm living an impoverished existence, God's Spirit reminds me that the Lord really is a stable, secure home for my life.

God's presence is a rich store of salvation and wisdom and knowledge. What else could I need that I don't find in him? Living with reverence for God and his ultimate reality opens these treasures to me.

God deeply desires grace for me because grace is who God is. I live in a world where what is called "love" is conditional, unpredictable, sometimes even overwhelming. Some who I wish would show me love may be unavailable. Some are oppressively available. But in all my ups and downs, my emotional highs and lows, God has been steadily and generously present. In so many ways, God persists in reminding me of this gracious invitation in my life. God enables me, if I'm open, to find inner courage to welcome and embrace this invitation.

God is moving toward me before I ever find myself drawn to God.

But instead, I sometimes choose anxiety as my basic response to life. Sometimes it looks like rehashing something that happened that I didn't like much. I replay what it might have been like if things had happened differently. Or I attempt to replay events with a bit of guilt or shame about how I *should* have responded (instead of how I did). This is fruitless activity that requires an immense amount of inner energy. What if I had those resources to invest in truly fruitful endeavors?

At other times, in my anxiety, I go over conversations I've had, or presentations I've given, or work I've done and try to improve them in my imagination. There may be something to be learned in such an activity, but I'm not usually seeking to learn as much as to over-correct myself for perceived failures.

It helps to recognize that how I respond to the challenges or hiccups that happen in my experience is something I can change. My anxious reactions and negative ruminations use up energy that is then unavailable to me in the only moment I am actually able to live—the present one. I end up using time and energy in a way that fails to be productive. I could instead use that time and energy in the present moment to engage my work with compassion, creativity, wisdom, and freedom in whatever opportunities lie immediately before me.

JESUS' VISION OF THE FATHER

Jesus wants to help me in this way of life. Jesus casts for me a vision of just how generous his Father is. In the upper room, Jesus told his inner circle that a day was coming when they would make requests of the Father in the name of Jesus. "In that day you will ask in my name. I am not saying that I will ask the Father on your behalf. No, the Father himself loves you because you have loved me and have believed that I came from God" (John 16:26-27).

Jesus wants us to know that the Father's posture toward us is generous. The intercession of Jesus is not about convincing the Father to see us differently than he does otherwise. The Father doesn't need to be convinced to be gracious with us. This vision of the Father quiets my anxieties.

Not only does Jesus not have to convince the Father to take a kinder approach with us, but we are the Father's generous gift to the Son. "I have revealed you to those whom you gave me out of the world. They were yours; you gave them to me and they have obeyed your word" (John 17:6). Gifts are things of value. Being made in the image of God is our value. Though that image may have been distorted or even damaged, we are God's masterpieces even if we are in need of some restoration. Such a masterpiece would still be a gift to an artist who knew its essential worth and had a vision to restore it. God has such a vision for us.

SCRUPULOSITY BLOCKS THE FLOW OF GRACE

When it comes to opponents of grace and peace, there is an old and perhaps unfamiliar word that describes a great challenge for many: *scrupulosity*. It can be understood as a sort of religious obsessive-compulsive disorder. It's a focus on moral minutiae and spiritual practice precision. In my case, it is a profound attention to details of doing everything right and cultivating a sharp eye for whenever I do something wrong.

It's probably not unlike Jesus' description of the Pharisees, who he observes, "You give a tenth of your spices—mint, dill and cumin. But you have neglected the more important matters of the law—justice, mercy, and faithfulness. You should have practiced the latter, without neglecting the former" (Matthew 23:23). Sadly, my focus on moral minutiae does not lead to a greater alignment with God, but usually to anxious care about my standing with God.

I have desperately needed the words of the prophet Jeremiah, "'No longer will they teach their neighbor, or say to one another, "Know the LORD," because they will all know me, from the least of them to the greatest,' declares the LORD. 'For I will forgive their wickedness and will remember their sins no more'" (Jeremiah 31:34). Jeremiah's description of the relationship the Father intends with us is much more than an obsessive focus on all my tiny observances. The arrangement Jeremiah describes is better, because instead of being dependent on the people's obedience to God's law, it will be rooted in God's transformation of our minds and hearts so that we know him and his ways.

I am touched by Jeremiah's words of mercy and grace, "I will forgive their wickedness and will remember their sins no more." God doesn't want to keep my wickedness in mind like I've tended to do. God wants to forgive. God is able to put our sins out of mind. He can do what I can't always seem to do with my own short-comings and offenses; even labeling my sins this way externalizes them and separates them from their relational realities. I've not only been breaking rules—I've been affecting a relationship.

But God is greater than my shortcomings. He is able and willing to forgive my offenses. It may be that there is no health in me apart from his grace (as the Anglican prayer of confession reminds me each morning), but I am not apart from his grace. I am showered with grace. I am soaking in grace. Grace is God's bias toward generosity, kindness, acceptance, and forgiveness in his way of relating to me. This is such good news.

I found a profoundly simple description of *scrupulosity* recently.

> In scrupulosity, a person's obsessions focus on moral or religious fears, such as the fear of being an evil person or the fear of divine retribution for sin. Although it can affect non-religious people, it is usually related to religious beliefs. In the strict sense, not all obsessive-compulsive behaviors related to religion are instances of scrupulosity: strictly speaking, for example, scrupulosity is not present in people who repeat religious requirements merely to be sure that they were done properly.[4]

I recognize this obsession with doing everything right. I find myself often focused on my weaknesses, my defects, my short-comings. Like the Pharisees, this has not borne the fruit of greater alignment with God, but has instead produced guilt and shame. God's strategy for enabling us to live more and more free from habits of sin is not condemnation. God invites me to gaze on his mercy and grace.

There isn't much power or freedom in being told, "You shouldn't sin anymore. You are bad because of what you've done or failed to do. You should do better." This sort of "shoulding" on ourselves does not empower us for better living. It keeps us trapped in our guilt and shame, which do not empower good or holy living. Anxiety thrives here.

My own scrupulosity is a continual racket in the back of my mind and in the depths of my soul. Because I can't seem to quiet it, my strategy tends to be to try to avoid it, escape it, or distract myself from it. This is an engine for many of the shortcomings or offenses that then scrupulosity grabs hold of to accuse me further. It's a vicious and hopeless cycle.

One of my great problems is that I've put my trust in scrupulosity. I've assumed it was serving a good purpose. It caused me to take my religious life seriously. I became very vigilant (maybe hypervigilant) about avoiding conscious wrongs or wounding of others. I came to feel that I was a mess when I came to Christ, and so I wanted to do things right. A good intention, but an unhelpful strategy. I thought it was creating a healthy reverence of God in me, but it seems instead to have made me afraid of God.

There is a difference between acknowledging my lack of growth in the presence of grace versus obsessing about my short-comings apart from a vision of grace. Scrupulosity functions like a self-improvement motor inside me, but self-improvement is not God's primary invitation in my life. It's a sort of least-common-denominator attempt at earning favor rather than a rich, abundant rightness with God in Christ.

God invites me to fill my vision of Jesus as the one who is full of grace and full of truth (John 1:14). The scrupulous voices of the Jewish leaders with whom Jesus had so many conflicts are like the voice in the back of my head. Jesus has a different voice. Scrupulosity hunts down my shortcomings. Jesus acknowledges them, but focuses on forgiveness, acceptance, and encouragement.

Scrupulosity is not my friend. It's a "reality distortion" voice. It is my dis-ease. It can't be reformed. What needs to be reformed (or awakened) is my true self in God, and my ability to accept and be hospitable to my whole self as God has made it. I must not let scrupulosity have more authority in my life than mercy and grace do. In an odd way, my scrupulosity seems to take certain sorts of offenses or failings *more* seriously than Jesus takes them. Jesus knows the harm that real sin does, but my obsession with little offenses might be doing more harm than those little offenses themselves. Jesus wants me instead to find my way forward in alignment with his peace, his joy, his hopefulness for me.

FOCUSING ON THE DON'TS

Another facet of how anxiety resists grace can be found in our wrestling with misaligned desires. In his letter to the Colossians, Paul speaks to the impulse to meet such desires with rules like "Do not handle! Do not taste! Do not touch!" (Colossians 2:21). Such rules seek to meet misaligned desire with the scarcity that comes from an attempt at absolute abstinence. Paul says that rules like this look wise, but are actually worthless when it comes to dealing with the reality of impulsive sensual desires. These "don't-oriented" approaches to life management unfortunately enjoy great job security because they appear appropriately serious and pious. The problem is that they don't address the root of the problem. They don't point us to true abundance that would be the answer to any temptation. It's very difficult to tempt a satisfied person.[5]

Instead of blocking desire with anxious rules, Paul invites us to focus and direct our hearts and minds—our emotional and mental energies—on things above (Colossians 3:1). Redirection rather than prohibition is what he recommends. A vision of abundance shines light on the emptiness of misdirected desires. These desires are to be transformed rather than banned, redirected rather than merely resisted. Bringing and keeping these impulses before God can transform them into what they were originally intended to be. And so holiness is not mainly a matter of saying "no" one hundred times, but rather a simple, sustained, and abundant "yes" to God.

This is a perspective I can grow in. My vision of God's fullness can be refreshed in prayer. Christ *is* in me. The fullness of God is in Christ, and the fullness of Christ is in me, bringing me to fullness (Colossians 2:9-10). I am still learning to more fully trust Christ in this reality.

It is my hope that you'll grow in a vision of God's grace and peace. May God's empowering presence, his measureless generosity, and his great goodness be with you, seeking you before ever you seek him. And may grace bear the fruit of deep well-being, freedom from anxious care, and a soul at rest in the presence of God our Father and the Lord Jesus Christ. Amen!

NON-ANXIOUS REFLECTION

+ In your experience, what relationship have you noticed between an awareness of God's generous, empowering presence (grace) and your own well-being in soul (peace)? Why not ask the Spirit to refresh a vision of the grace of God-with-you?

- Anxiety is usually aimed at surviving. Grace invites us to thriving. How have you experienced these two ways of living? How might God's generosity be inviting you to thrive more in this very season of life in which you find yourself?

- In what ways do you identify with the challenge of scrupulosity? What have been some of your personal programs of trying hard to appear righteous? What fruit have they borne?

5

PRACTICING PRESENCE

Gem and I were at the airport ready to depart for Chicago. We were about thirty minutes from boarding, and I was looking through my briefcase when I realized my computer wasn't in there. My computer is my traveling office. It's where I keep all my speaking notes. You can imagine my first reaction to this discovery was not very peaceful. I found it easy to accuse myself of yet another absentminded moment. Along with a wash of familiar adrenaline came a rapid-fire series of thoughts:

- *How in the world am I going to give my talks?*

- *This is going to be an absolute disaster. How could I have been so stupid.* (I've sadly too often found it quite easy to be self-accusing.)

- *What in the world am I going to do? I don't have time to drive the fifty-minute round trip home to get my computer and still catch this flight!*

Other thoughts like these continued to ratchet up my anxiety. But then, unexpectedly, another thought bubbled up into my consciousness. It sounded like this: *I wonder how this just might work out better than I expect.* It rang with the encouraging tone of Psalm 23, "The LORD is my shepherd. I lack nothing."

What I had been practicing in that season was answering my anxious thoughts and feelings with the reality of God's shepherding presence. My anxiety, being a poor predictor of the future, was looking into my next few days and forecasting disaster. But anxiety doesn't recognize the presence of a Shepherd in our future.

Within moments, I realized that all my important documents, including notes for all the talks I had prepared, were stored safely in the internet cloud, and that Gem had not forgotten her computer like I had. I would be able to access everything I needed after all.

PRACTICING PRESENCE, PRACTICING ABSENCE

A beautiful remedy to my frequent anxious feelings is remembering that God is with me—practicing God's presence. It's good for me to remember that the deepest thirst of my life is for God. How long can we survive without friendship? Perhaps months or even years. How long can we survive without food? Perhaps weeks. How long can we survive without water? Perhaps days. How long can we survive without air? Perhaps minutes. How long can we survive without the presence of God? Not even one moment. And rather than a statement in the negative, we can hear this as a welcome invitation to live every single moment in the presence of God and his abundant kingdom.

My deepest thirsts are filled in God. When I live my life and conduct myself driven by anxiety, I am forgetting God's generous, refreshing presence. I imagine that I won't have enough of what I need to live or work well, or that it may run out at any moment. I imagine my efforts will turn out poorly. Anxiety only has power over me when I trust its voice and follow its constricting counsel.

Practicing the presence of God and practicing the presence of anxiety train me in opposite directions. When I practice the presence of my anxious feelings, it ends up as an exercise in practicing the absence of God. My feelings of anxiety do not force me to worry about my worry. I can learn to acknowledge that a feeling of anxiety has been provoked by something that has happened or by a thought that has arisen. I can say to myself, *Ah yes. This is what it's like when I feel worried. But my worry has not been a reliable indicator of my reality in God's presence. It is a feeling I need not ignore, but I also don't want to offer it the steering wheel of my life.*

My anxiety has little awareness of the presence of God-with-me, who that God is, and how that God relates to me. If I let it, anxiety encloses me in a small bubble of self-engrossing rumination. Inside this bubble, my thoughts feel like a swarm of flies in my head. My worry is a sort of meditation in the negative. When I worry, I find myself ruminating about what should have happened, or what might happen, or what isn't going to happen the way I want. A remedy for me is to learn to contemplate the reality of God-with-me, instead of anxiety's suggested topics.

EMBODIED OR DISEMBODIED

This dynamic of meditation is not just a cognitive activity. It isn't merely using my mind differently. Meditation involves my God-given body. My body is a dwelling place of the very presence of God's Spirit (1 Corinthians 6:19). Anxiety has a way of becoming embedded in our physical selves. The energies of trauma can get stuck in our bodies and provoke a great deal of anxious feeling. I've discovered that I cannot just think my way out of anxious moods. There is a way of engaging my body that is a divine invitation to presence and peace.

Another way to say this is that anxiety often feels like an out-of-body experience. I don't mean that in a sort of mystical sense, but more literally. My anxiety is an impulse to seek to be present in the past or in the future rather than in the present. And my body is only here in the present. This might seem rather simplistic, but it's become a rather important piece of wisdom for me.

Practicing the presence of my body in the present moment with God has been important for me. It's been an avenue for experiencing the classic practice of the presence of God that Brother Lawrence spoke of.[1] It's a way of experiencing the fruit of how centering prayer might guide me.

What does this look like? I may sit in a comfortable, firm chair that supports my back well. I'll settle my feet in front of me in a comfortable position. I then begin to pay attention to what I'm feeling in my body. Does it feel more like anxiety or more like peace? Maybe my forehead feels tense. Maybe my brain feels blurry. My low back might be a bit tight. My stomach or chest might have some discomfort or tightness I often identify as anxious feelings.

Whatever I notice, I will usually seek to acknowledge God present with me through relaxed and deep breathing. I love that one of the biblical metaphors for the Spirit of God is breath. I imagine breathing the very presence of the Spirit into those places in me that feel out of alignment, stressed, tight, or uncomfortable. I imagine the Spirit realigning me, unburdening me, relaxing me, quieting me, comforting me. God is even more present to me than the various physical sensations I experience. I often feel the effect of this in my body becoming more relaxed overall. And I feel more present in my body, which enables me to be more present in the moment in which I find myself.

Sometimes, after I've noticed places of particular concern, I'll do a scan of my body from the top of my head to my feet. I'll seek to welcome the presence of God into the whole of my body. I may imagine my body as God's temple being made a bit more real to me (perhaps we could say "real-ized"). I find that my lived experience of trust deepens. Anxiety withers in the presence of trust. Focusing on the reliable and caring presence of God-with-me and for me strikes at the root of worry. Envisioning the loving presence of God-with-me, by the Spirit in my very body, often answers the frantic ruminations of worry.

BELONGING TO GOD

As I remember who I am, learning to live more in the way of God's peace has been enriched. It helps when I remember that my identity, purpose, and value is rooted in my Maker. One of the Psalms that I enjoy most mornings when I pray is Psalm 100. I love rehearsing these lines:

> Be assured that the LORD, he is God;
>> it is he that has made us, and not we ourselves;
>> we are his people, and the sheep of his pasture.
>> (Psalm 100:3 BCP 2019)

Uncertainty about my value and purpose in life produces a lot of anxiety. The Lord is God, not me. To some ears, that may sound somehow limiting or devaluing. I find those words freeing and empowering. This God made me—made us. We are not the architects of our own lives. We have not made ourselves. It's good to remember that. Who we are is seen most clearly in remembering how we have come to be. We belong to God like a beloved child belongs to a parent.

Being the sheep of his pasture means that he is committed to our care, our protection, and our good. As my confidence grows in God as the One who made me and cares most for me, confidence and peace replace timidity and anxiety. When I imagine that my sense of worth or purposes is completely left up to me, instead of freedom I find myself overwhelmed.

If I transfer my sense of identity from my own self-establishment to the opinion of others about me, then my sense of worth is dependent on their assessment of me. I have sometimes found it hard to step off this identity treadmill. I do whatever it takes to keep people thinking well of me. I found that I couldn't say no when that was probably my best response to an expectation or request. Do you hear the anxiety in all this? Anxiety is a displacement of trust from a reliable God to my own unreliable ideas, expectations, beliefs, and self-definitions, and those of others.

PEACE AS A PERSON

I think of Jesus' disciples hiding behind locked doors on the day Jesus was raised, anxious about what the Jewish leaders might do to them (John 20:19). The disciples were unpracticed in resurrection; they were only just becoming *aware* of resurrection. It would be a while before those first followers became practiced in the realities of resurrection, before they grew more and more rooted in a life that arises from death.

Jesus spoke to them of these things in the upper room. He told them, "Before long, the world will not see me anymore, but you will see me. Because I live, you also will live. On that day you will realize that I am in my Father, and you are in me, and I am in you. Whoever has my commands and keeps them is the one who loves me. The one who loves me will be loved by my Father, and I too will love them and show myself to them" (John 14:19-21).

Jesus was aware of his coming death and burial. The disciples weren't, and so resurrection was beyond their imagination at that moment. Very soon, the world would not see him as they had for three years or so. The disciples were going to witness his death, burial, and then resurrection and ascension. They did not know what this meant at this moment. Jesus risen will mean them risen, and means us risen. There is a moment of realization that Jesus is in his Father, and that we are in him, and he is in us. This is, again, the closest of relationships to which he invites us.

I hear these words and want them to come alive in me. I want to realize more deeply that Jesus is united with the Father, that Jesus is in me and I in him. There is a peace in such a moment of trustful awareness. There have been moments along the way when I realized more deeply and fully the reality of Father and Son, mutually dwelling together in the Spirit. I am trustfully aware of that reality more today than I was five or ten years ago.

This peaceful union isn't like knowing something I read in a book. It is the knowledge of loving encounter and intimate interaction. It is a relational knowing. It is the knowing of real presence. It is the experience of living mercy and grace, of God making himself known to me right in the middle of my shortcomings and offenses.

Old habits of hiding, escaping, avoiding, and numbing have sorely tempted me in recent years. But these are not paths to peace; they aren't a way to choose life. Those paths avoid discomfort rather than finding comfort engaging in fellowship with the Prince of Peace.

Returning to the post-resurrection scene when Jesus comes to be among his inner circle, his first gift is to come and stand among them. He simply gives them the gift of his presence—his risen presence. He stands with them in the place of their many worries. The door that is locked in fear does not prevent the loving, joyful, peace-bringing presence of Jesus to be among them. And what is the first thing he says to his anxious, fearful disciples? He says, "Peace be with you!" He actually says those words twice, as though they need the gift of reinforcement (John 20:19, 21).

Might not Jesus speak the words, "Peace be with you," as many times as we need as well? This could help us awaken more fully to the presence of the risen Christ among us. We could find ourselves animated more and more by the peaceful, risen presence of Christ among us—Christ in us.

The risen Christ speaks peace to us all the time: It's a deep-rooted peace. A real peace. A substantial peace. A personal peace. This peace is the very atmosphere of his kingdom reign. Peace really *is* with us. Peace *really will be* with us. In fearful, anxious times and situations, *peace* companions us and accompanies us. We will not be abandoned to what threatens us.

And the peace of God is a Person. That Person is an absolute *Prince* of Peace. Peace is the way of Jesus. In our anxious times, let's remain awake and attentive to these good words of Jesus: "Peace be with you!" May they come to echo in our hearts and minds day by day.

Elsewhere, Paul the apostle encourages us to find life in Christ who is risen. "Since, then, you have been raised with Christ, set your hearts on things above, where Christ is, seated at the right hand of God. Set your minds on things above, not on earthly things. For you died, and your life is now hidden with Christ in God. When Christ, who is your life, appears, then you also will appear with him in glory" (Colossians 3:1-4).

There is an insight that brought life to Paul that he shared with his friends in a little town called Colossae. This basic and living reality is that Christ is risen, and that we are risen with him. He wanted them (and us) to realize that life is not made up merely of the realities of their challenges, their troubles, or their responsibilities. In the midst of these realities there is Reality. We really are raised and seated with Christ at the Father's right hand. Our lives are rooted there. We engage earthly realities with kingdom abundance and confidence.

This risenness with Christ enables us to live with a sense of settled favor and rooted authority. We don't live in a kingdom struggling to survive. The presence of God is a place of measureless abundance and great generosity. God is for us so that nothing that seeks our harm will have the final say. This is the nature of our kingdom authority. This is a place of peaceful power.

There is a way of seeing the challenging or even overwhelming realities of our lives against the backdrop of Christ's real presence. We do not need to treat these ground-level realities as ultimate realities. They do not represent the source of our life. They are the place in which we express our life. That life is sourced in the life of God in us and among us. I don't go looking for my life in the midst of earthly realities. I go to express life I already have. I bring life—God's life—to the world around me. This isn't about making me the focus. This simply makes me a conduit through which God can bless the world God loves.

Perhaps even more simply stated: Christ *is* our life. Paul isn't merely saying that Jesus Christ rose from the dead as a historical fact or a theological truth. Christ is risen and alive among us today. Eternal life is not a someday hope. It is a today actuality. Right now, as you read the words on this page, Jesus is risen with you.

You are risen with him. He was with you before you picked up this book to read a few more pages. He will be with you in whatever you do next. In this way, Christ is alive and present to guide you, encourage you, energize you, companion you. The Prince of Peace is right here and right now.

CLINGING

I've discovered that if I am clinging to my worries, I am not clinging to the Prince of Peace. I don't write that sentence as an expression of guilt or shame. It is, to my mind, simply a statement of fact. A light switch is on or off. That's how anxiety works in my experience. It is a mode of life in which my awareness of God-with-me in favor and care simply isn't my operating system. There is a difference between clinging to my worries and casting my worries into the hands of my Father in heaven.

I can cling to my worries and have ideas about God, but that's not the same as living in communion with the God of peace. I can give my attention to the voice of worry in me, or I can give my attention to the voice of the Spirit of peace within me. I cannot let them both be my guide in the same moment. And one tends to be a tyrant while the other calls himself a good shepherd.

Reminding myself of my reasons to pivot away from worry toward the God who cares for me has a way of exposing the emptiness of the dire predictions anxiety whispers. Reminding myself of how well cared for I really am relieves the pressure of the cares that anxiety points to without reference to the care of God.

When I sink into the presence of God where there is peace, joy, hope, and kindness, my anxieties tend to burn off like a morning marine layer here in Southern California. My anxiety and depression are lightened and lifted in the presence of divine joy and peace. My despair is cut through by the light of God's hopeful presence. My worries about a God watching for a chance to punish me or reject me will melt in the presence of everlasting kindness.

This way of practicing the presence of God could be called a contemplative life. Author and spiritual director Thomas Green said that a contemplative attitude is when God is no longer "he," but "you."[2] God is inviting us to be contemplative leaders, men and women of influence who follow Jesus closely and work with God as "you," rather than working *for* God as "him."

Psychiatrist and theologian Gerald May once asked, "Why, when everything around me is perfect and I am immersed in the moment, do I still think I must *do* something to be contemplative? It is always only by a gift that I am allowed to just be. Left to my own devices, I will always be trying to do something—even if what I am trying to do is nothing."[3]

Practicing God's presence, seeking to live a more contemplative life, is not something separate from me that I'm trying to achieve. There is really nothing closer at hand than living a contemplative life. My frantic efforts to do this, though, move me away from God-with-me in the present moment. The contemplative life is about as hard as waking up from sleep. But it is a grace in that I can't wake myself up without help. I need the help of God to live a deep-rooted life at home in him.

There is a light breeze blowing in our backyard just now. The rigid frame of our wooden patio cover doesn't budge. But grass and bushes and trees are all waving in the wind. Let's let ourselves be moved by the wind of God's Spirit today. Let's learn from Jesus how to be more supple, attentive, receptive, and responsive to every divine movement. May we learn to be led by the Spirit of

God in our every moment. This is how Jesus lived, and he's invited us to be his students. May you grow more and more aware and confident in the real presence of God-with-you.

NON-ANXIOUS REFLECTION

- How do you feel about the idea that worrying is a way of practicing the absence of God? Does it ring true? How would you like to practice God's presence with you in moments of anxious thoughts and feelings? Why not ask God's help in this?

- Feel the tangible reality in your hands of the book you are reading, whether in print or on a device; it is there. What does it mean to you that God is even more present to you than this book? Give yourself a few moments to take in this reality.

- How do you feel about the idea that peace is a Person—the Prince of Peace? You could take a few moments to remind yourself in prayer, "You are with me, Prince of Peace. I am with you here and now. Thank you." Feel free to repeat this prayer more than once if it helps you.

6

SIMPLE VIRTUES

Our hyperconnected world is adding immensely to our anxiety. If we are on social media, we may be aware of being watched. We may feel pushed to impress. Many of us feel we're losing the comparison battle. We're tempted to curate our public image to maximum benefit. Whether we feel we're succeeding or failing in this endeavor, it's a lot of pressure.

What if instead we let a voice very different from this social media instinct guide us into the simpler ways of humility, gentleness, patience, dependence, or even surrender? Many of these words may sound uninviting, but we might discover that aiming at being smaller is a better way to live than always trying to be bigger. It's good for us to remember that in the presence of an almighty God, we actually *are* small and this might be good news.

This voice guiding us into the small way might sound like Paul urging us to interact with one another as Jesus did. Fully God, Jesus doesn't cling to his privilege but instead makes himself nothing, even servant-like; he humbles himself all the way to the cross (Philippians 2:5-8). In a sense, Jesus starts at the absolute biggest place in all creation, and then he takes the very smallest place as a human being, coming as a servant and serving us in loving sacrifice. This is the path the Prince of Peace chooses. This is the path on which we best learn to follow him.

LIVE JESUS!

One of the guides in this simple way that I've appreciated over the years is Francis de Sales, a seventeenth-century bishop and spiritual guide who, together with his friend Jane de Chantal, encouraged his friends to "Live Jesus." I love their gracious way of guiding souls. There is a peaceful and peaceable way about it. Theirs was a gentle approach to spiritual formation that was helpful in the tumultuous season of the Protestant Reformation. He highlighted for us what he liked to call the "little virtues."

Our instinct is often to seek impressive virtues, exciting virtues, even heroic virtues. What if those virtues that are held in highest regard in the kingdom of God are actually humility and gentleness, among others? This is what we hear in the invitation of Jesus who describes himself as gentle and humble in heart (Matthew 11:29). Practicing these simple virtues right-sizes my life.

Pursuing theses little virtues will not lead to a small life. The little virtues are the way of Jesus, and so they are the way of growth in the glory and the power of God's kingdom. Peace grows well in the soil of these simple virtues.

The community of sisters that Francis and Jane founded were called the Visitandines, named for the event of Mary's visit to Elizabeth in Luke 1. It's out of this visit that we witness Mary's beautiful prayer of loving, humble submission to God's calling in her life (Luke 1:46-55). This community of sisters "were to grow in love by 'Living Jesus' among themselves, by allowing their own hearts to be hollowed out by the practice of what Jane and Francis called the little virtues. Not everyone might be called to practice the heroic virtues, or asked to perform great works, but all could do little things with great love. Thus humility, patience, simplicity, kindness, and gentleness would be the virtues that the Visitandine sisters would cultivate."[1]

Their vision of "living Jesus" was simple and humble, hollowing out their hearts. Does this sound like emptiness? Their vision seems to have been to open up space in their souls for Jesus to be more at home in them. Wouldn't the Jesus who is gentle and humble in heart be more at home in a gentle and humble heart?

There is a calm peace that grows in the spaciousness of hearts that have been hollowed out by simple virtues like humility, patience, simplicity, kindness, and gentleness. These are certainly not popular virtues in the world around us. There is something in us that may feel the need to be spiritually heroic, but in my own journey that has usually looked less like honoring God and more like wanting to be seen as spiritually impressive.

We often resist empty space, especially if it is a big empty space within us. But sometimes, for a season, we may feel more empty than full, more thirsty than quenched, more hungry than satisfied. Usually the season does not last forever. (Sometimes, there may be a unique call to identify with the suffering of Jesus, which Paul described as a desire in his heart. Mother Teresa deeply identified with Jesus' experience of thirsting through her own years- and decades-long experiences of God's felt absence more than felt presence.) We're invited to a trusted fullness sometimes through a lack of felt fullness. This is space for the Prince of Peace to be more at home in us. One of David's prayers captures the peaceful spirit of this simple way:

My heart is not proud, LORD,
    my eyes are not haughty;

I do not concern myself with great matters
    or things too wonderful for me.
But I have calmed and quieted myself,
    I am like a weaned child with its mother;
    like a weaned child I am content. (Psalm 131:1-2)

Whether David prayed this before he was king, while being pursued by Saul, or prayed it *as* king, he expresses his intention to resist pride. He aims not at great matters but simple ones. He isn't trying to be wonderful in front of others. What fruit does such a prayer produce in David? David's heart grows calm and quiet when he isn't trying to impress everyone else. He is like a weaned child with his mother: instead of seeing mother only as a source of desperately needed nourishment, a weaned child finds contentment in the company of mother.

There is peace in this posture for David and for us. We can learn that we don't need to live impressive lives. We don't have to spend any time thinking about how everyone else sees us. We don't have to appear wonderful to others. We can live in a posture of calm, quiet contentment in the presence of God.

HUMILITY

One of the virtues foreign to conventional wisdom is humility. Today, pride is promoted as a virtue. It is sometimes overt, and at other times implicit. This is perhaps because people misunderstand what humility is. What it *isn't* is devaluing or demeaning. It isn't thinking of yourself as a nothing. It is experiencing the peace and relief of not thinking about yourself nearly as much. Saint Mark the Ascetic, a fifth century monk, suggested that "humility consists, not in condemning our conscience, but in recognizing

God's grace and compassion."[2] Humility is what being God-saturated looks like.

Peter connects peace and humility in his first letter: "Humble yourselves, therefore, under God's mighty hand, that he may lift you up in due time. Cast all your anxiety on him because he cares for you" (1 Peter 5:6-7). It's good for us to connect the invitation to throw our cares into the caring hands of God with actively living humbly under God's mighty hand. You can learn to "live carefree before God; he is most careful with you" (1 Peter 5:7 MSG).

Humility and peace are easy companions. Pride and anxiety are, unfortunately, close associates as well. When I try to take responsibility for what is God's alone to care for, I find myself anxious. This sort of anxiety is a symptom of a mistaken level of personal sovereignty. It is proud to imagine that I can completely control situations and people to protect myself from potential harm. I may not see it as pride at the time, but it's pride just the same. Pride imagines that the only one who can care well for me is *me*. Humility recognizes the faithful care of God-with-me.

When I humbly trust God's powerful care, I am putting myself under God's strong protection. God cares for me. God does not necessarily keep bad things from happening to me; we all know that from experience. But God is not overwhelmed by the bad things that happen to me, and is able to help me navigate these things with humble courage. He listens with compassion to my sad, fearful, or even angry prayers.

I appreciate the word Peter uses about what to do with my worries. I *cast* them on God. It's a Greek word that would have been used to describe someone throwing a burden onto an animal to carry instead. I throw my worries on God's pile rather than letting them pile up in my heart and mind. He bears the weight of them rather than me trying to do so. My problem is that sometimes I cast my cares on God, but then I reel them back in.

Rather than clinging to my anxieties by mulling them over, ruminating about them, running multiple future scenarios of potentially painful outcomes that I really cannot predict or guarantee, I can release them, cast them, into God's caring hands. We cast our anxieties on God because God *is* love. Rather than being irresponsible, this is being rightly responsible. I am taking the responsibility that is mine and releasing the responsibility that was never given to me.

Peter reminds us that we don't exalt ourselves, mindless of God's might. Instead, we humble ourselves under God's mighty (and very gracious) hand. Humility is merely the truest response to kingdom reality. He is King. I am not. When we humble ourselves in God, God is then free to *give* us authority and favor ("lift us up") in due time. He has the wisdom to know when that is. We almost always think we're ready sooner than he does. He is preparing us for the good things he wants to give and to do through us.

I wonder if a variety of "exalting ourselves" rather than humbling ourselves is found in the old idea of *vainglory*. It's not a word we use much today, but it is simply (and literally) "empty fame." There is true glory in that which is good, beautiful, and true in a human life. But empty glory is managing our appearances to persuade others to think highly of us. Instead of remembering that our value—our glory—is given, we outsource our identity to the reactions of others. Social media is a playground for vainglory, and anxiety is the ever-present bully. It can be exhausting to curate a bigger-than-life on-screen identity. The unreality of vainglory fosters anxiety.

We don't have to unknowingly hand over to others the keys to our sense of meaning, value, and importance. When we seek glory in achievement, acquisition, and accolades, we learn too late that this is empty. Our identity and value are not nearly as fragile as that. There isn't anything for us in empty fame, unfounded reputation, meaningless "influence." Our true glory is reflecting the glory of God. We learn to think less about ourselves (humility) and more about God (praise), and we grow in true beauty.

GENTLENESS

There is another virtue alongside humility that Jesus specifically uses to describe himself. The simple virtue that is a good friend to humility and peace is *gentleness*. Jesus adds this virtue to humility in his well-known words about finding rest for our souls in him: "Come to me, all you who are weary and burdened, and I will give you rest. Take my yoke upon you and learn from me, for I am gentle and humble in heart, and you will find rest for your souls. For my yoke is easy and my burden is light" (Matthew 11:28-30). Gentleness and humility are an easy yoke to carry. Harshness and pride are an anxious and burdensome one.

Saint Mark the Ascetic tells us that the one "who is gentle in God's sight is wiser than the wise; and [the one] who is humble in heart is stronger than the strong. For they bear the yoke of Christ with spiritual knowledge."[3] This equation of gentleness with wisdom, and humility with strength, is not a popular one in our current cultural climate. But this is the nature of the kingdom of God. This is the way of Jesus. And this is a way to be at home in peace.

When we bear the easy yoke of Jesus, the one who is gentle and humble in heart, we find rest for our worries. In this humble, gracious peace we learn to be gentle with ourselves. Francis de Sales uses the image of a father's correction to help us learn this.

> A father's gentle, loving rebuke has far greater power to correct a child than rage and passion. So too when we have committed some fault if we rebuke our heart by a calm, mild remonstrance, with more compassion for it than passion against it and encourage it to make amendment, then repentance conceived in this way will sink far deeper and penetrate more effectually than fretful, angry, stormy repentance.[4]

I've made the mistake before of thinking that if I'm especially hard on myself, my behavior will improve. But Francis suggests that it is actually more true that treating ourselves with gentleness and kindness will cause much deeper and more lasting change in us.[5] And peace will attend this change.

I remember once when I was working my way through some daily details, and I went to update my credit card information on a website and discovered that my primary credit card was not in my wallet. I then noticed that my driver's license wasn't there either. I couldn't remember what I'd done with them. I felt panic!

I began to experience a series of thoughts about worst-case scenarios: of the card being misused to run up a massive credit card balance, or the great inconvenience of having to replace my driver's license at the DMV. Panic like this shuts down my creative, higher thinking capacities. I couldn't then think well about what might have happened to my credit card and license.

Of course, I did the practical thing of checking my credit card account online for any transactions that weren't mine. I checked the last charge that I knew was mine and called to see if I might have left my card there. No help. I've been learning, though, to remind myself that God really is my shepherd, and that I am not going to find myself in a situation of lack. I've sometimes rehearsed that as "This just might turn out better than I assume."

As I stopped fretting and ruminating and let myself rest in God's care and provision, even if I had indeed lost my card and license, I suddenly had a recollection of cycling over the weekend. I remembered putting my license and my credit card in my cycling jersey as ID and payment in case I needed it. I checked that jersey, and there they were. But in the past I've let something like this episode paralyze me as I obsessed about the terrible possible futures that lay before me. The gentler approach of trust has led to far more peace.

I probably won't ever reach a point when anxious feelings do not arise in me. But I can learn to recognize anxiety before it roots itself in my thoughts and my will. I can respond differently to the anxious feelings that still arise uninvited into my awareness. I've already learned that I don't have to hand over the steering wheel of my life decisions to everything anxiety whines, complains, or shouts its dire warnings about.

Wendy Wright, a leading expert on the spirituality of Francis de Sales and his friends, unpacks Francis's vision of Jesus as gentle and humble.

> "Come to Me," he declares, "and learn from Me for I am gentle and humble of heart." God's kingdom realised is thus seen in this gentle, humble heart that confounds and overturns the values of the accepted order. It is not power over others, self-assertion or wealth that characterise God's reign, but love of God and neighbour exercised through all the

intimate, relational virtues like gentleness and humility. Salesian discipleship is thus first and foremost about an exchange of hearts. It is about the practice of "living Jesus" through the cultivation of the little relational virtues.[6]

It is the gentle, humble way of Jesus that overcomes the world. His way of bringing about change was subversive. He modeled the way of God's reign in the lives of people. They then became imitators of this gracious, kind way of living wherever they went. Everyone seemed to notice this difference. In the end, this is the lasting influence of the one who is humble and gentle in heart.

PATIENCE

In a culture where hurry is a virtue, impatience is seen as its necessary companion. The freeways in Southern California where I live feel like a NASCAR event. People are angered if they are inconvenienced on the scale of a nanosecond.

Again, Francis de Sales offers a different, more patient vision of life: "Undertake all your affairs with a calm mind and try to dispatch them in order one after the other. If you make an effort to do them all at once or without order, your spirits will be so overcharged and depressed that they will likely sink under the burden without effecting anything."[7]

Hurry and impatience assume that what needs to happen next is completely in my solitary control. But a vision of life in the kingdom assumes that God is present and always at work. Patience enables us to peacefully discern how God is present and what God may be doing. Patience learns to collaborate with God in life and work. This is King David's experience, as we hear in his prayer.

Be still before the Lord
    and wait patiently for him;
do not fret when people succeed in their ways,
    when they carry out their wicked schemes. (Psalm 37:7)

Patience here looks like stillness and unweary waiting. This is an inner posture we learn to cultivate. It is rooted in the expectation that God is present and working in grace, peace, and power. Impatience may seem to win the day, but such wins are temporary. Impatience rushes ahead, but rarely with a clear and good vision of where it is going. Impatience doesn't grow good roots. Patience does.

Consider the simple, potent counsel of James: "My dear brothers and sisters, take note of this: Everyone should be quick to listen, slow to speak and slow to become angry, because human anger does not produce the righteousness that God desires" (James 1:19-20). Some things should be done quickly. Some things should be slow. Being quick to listen is always good. When we listen, we learn. We gain wisdom and perspective. We come to understand one another so that we can speak with more truth and grace. We respond to people rather than wedging our own message in between their words. When we listen quicker than we speak, then we are wise and we live in love toward others. Such patient attention is a peaceful way to live.

When we speak too quickly and fail to listen, we often misunderstand the other, and we can quickly become angry. This is a common experience that many of us never realize we're having. We think we're angry at what is really happening, when we are actually angry about something we assume is happening but isn't. Impatience jumps to conclusions. Human anger does not lead us in God's good ways.

Patience makes us more attentive to kingdom realities in the midst of our everyday engagements. We learn to be quicker to listen to God in our work. We learn to listen even when we are speaking. We learn to listen to the heart that underlies the words of others. Patient listening fosters the fruit of peace more than impatient reacting.

Patience is the very first description of love Paul offers in his list of the qualities of love in 1 Corinthians 13:4. So, anxious impatience isn't compatible with love. Anxiety and true concern are different from each other. I've had many experiences along the way of seeing love and fretting equated: "You don't care if you don't frantically worry." Patience is a beautiful path to truly caring for the people in your life.

THE RISING TIDE

Once, on personal retreat, I was sitting in silence with an Atlantic bay before me. This ocean was a mirror reverse image of my usual Pacific Ocean vision. Here, the sun rises from the horizon instead of setting there. As I contemplated the scene before me, I found my soul at rest in God's presence. This isn't always how I feel, but I did then. It was a gift of grace and not something I achieved. Too often, I overestimate my own achievements and their worth.

Before me, I saw three small seabirds swimming toward me with their wakes interweaving. Such a beautiful but momentary work of art; so much of beauty is only momentary. Perhaps no one will notice it; it's humble and gentle. God enjoys making beauty, even if no one sees it. It is in God's nature as Creator. Noticing and taking in beauty is a place of peace for my soul.

During that retreat, I observed that the tidal range there was far greater than at home. At one point, the tide went from minus-one foot to plus-ten feet in about six hours: that's almost two feet per hour of change. I could sit and literally watch the tide slowly rise.

I saw harbor seals getting ready to lose their barely surfaced thrones to the tide. As the tide rose, I saw less and less of one seal's stone perch. The rock he was basking on was being slowly reclaimed by the bay. The tide was unhurried; in any one moment, it was hard to perceive the change. I saw a few small waves jostle my friend the seal, but he remained enthroned.

The slow surge of the tide felt like the sometimes imperceptible grace of God rising in my life. I can see changes if I compare one moment to a later one, or one season to another. But if I am still long enough, if I linger, I might perceive the slow, steady, faithful rising of the tide of God's love, God's grace, God's life in *my* life.

The gentle, humble strength of the rising tide is an image of Jesus to me. He is so mighty, so strong, that he has nothing to prove. He is perfectly content and secure in the Father's affection, delight, and purpose for him.

So days of retreat like these are not about making something happen through my many spiritual disciplines (reading, receiving Eucharist, writing in my journal, taking prayer walks, and such). They are an opportunity to slow down enough to notice the reliable rising of the tide of God's grace and peace. I want to learn to trust that grace rises even when I can't perceive it.

Becoming a student of Jesus will take us on the pathway of humility, gentleness, and patience. Learning these may involve challenging training. But it is training that will lead to a life of deeper peace and serenity. In the next chapter, we'll talk about two more little virtues that may prove to be strong medicine for our deep anxieties.

NON-ANXIOUS REFLECTION

- What is your honest first response to little virtues like gentleness, humility, or patience? What draws you to them? What within you resists them?

- How do you feel about the motto of Francis de Sales and his friends to "Live Jesus!"? What might it look and feel like to lean into this as a simple statement of your own life's purpose? How do you find it inviting?

- Think about Jesus for a moment. In what ways does your gut image of Jesus look gentle and humble in heart (Matthew 11:29)? In what ways do you imagine him instead as more impatient, demanding, or dissatisfied with you? Why not talk with him about this?

7

UNEXPECTED PATHS
TO PEACE

Walking the path of peace may take us in some
unfamiliar directions that don't seem all that inviting at first. Two
dynamics that have been an important part of my own journey
of coming to deeper peace of soul have been dependence and
surrender. Many would prefer independence and personal au-
tonomy. There is, of course, a *holy* independence that enables us
to be fully empowered to come to others as a servant. Holy
service requires confidence and strength. Ironically, this sort of
inner strength is more the fruit of surrender than it is of self-
promotion or self-improvement.

There is also an *unholy* independence that fails to acknowledge
need of anyone and anything; something in me resists the idea
that I might have needs. I don't want to need anyone or anything.
But I am not an autonomous being. I need food and water. I need
air. I need friendship. I need love. I need mercy and grace. I am
more dependent than I realize. This does not rob me of agency or
initiative, but it places those in a context. The Lord God is sovereign; I'm not. Recognizing this reality has proven to bring rest
to my soul.

A MISGUIDED OFFERING

I'm reminded of the words of Samuel after Saul had been caught making an offering that he wasn't authorized to make. He was supposed to have waited a week for Samuel to arrive, but he grew impatient and decided to do what he thought was needed. Samuel responds to Saul:

> Does the LORD delight in burnt offerings and sacrifices
>   as much as in obeying the LORD?
> To obey is better than sacrifice,
>   and to heed is better than the fat of rams.
> For rebellion is like the sin of divination,
>   and arrogance like the evil of idolatry.
>   (1 Samuel 15:22-23)

Samuel contrasts the good of obedience with the possibility that one might make heroic but self-serving sacrifices. Pride loves making impressive sacrifices, even if they don't align with God's guidance. They make pride look good. Better for us when we simply listen to God's guidance and align ourselves with his invitation to join him in it. Trusting the wisdom of God's guidance enables us to live in concert with his purposes. We find ourselves less at odds with how things actually are in the kingdom of God. To obey is to say, "You know what you're talking about, God, and there's nothing better for me than to trust your wisdom and follow your way."

These verses come in the context of Saul's decision to offer a sacrifice that Samuel was supposed to offer rather than waiting the full seven days Samuel had asked him to wait for his return. Here, offering the necessary sacrifice in the wrong way was not good. Obeying God's guidance was.

Considering the way of obedience made Saul nervous. He felt out of control. This is probably because obedience, by design, removes us from the position of final control. Saul chose to offer a sacrifice because that kept him feeling in control. This is why some will choose great sacrifice as a way of covering over deep disobedience. But this isn't a way of peace. Sacrifice can glorify human will rather than honoring God's good pleasure. Obedience is a loving offering of the human will. There is no amount of sacrifice that makes up for disobedience—they are not in the same accounting system.

We seem to imagine that we'll find more peace if we try to control outcomes and assert our own preferences. But Francis de Sales's friend, Jane de Chantal, has words to a friend about this perspective: "What God, in His goodness, asks of you is not this excessive zeal which has reduced you to your present condition, but a calm, peaceful uselessness, a resting near Him with no special attention or action of the understanding of will except a few words of love, or of faithful, simple surrender, spoken softly, effortlessly, without the least desire to find consolation or satisfaction in them."[1]

Jane's friend is engaging her life with a kind of excessive zeal that has exhausted and overwhelmed her. Her way has led her to an anxious life. Jane suggests something that sounds odd to our contemporary sensitivities: try a calm, peaceful uselessness in God's presence.

Don't try so hard with God.

Receive what God is giving.

Enter into what God is doing.

Offer a simple expression of your love to God.

Be as gentle with yourself as God is.

Don't come to God only to feel better.
Welcome however God wishes to be present.
This is a way of peace.

THE GREATEST LOVE

There is an odd spiritual independence that seems to think that our loving of God is more important than God's loving of us. Reading that sentence, you probably don't actually believe it, but our actions can speak louder than our professions. In a letter to a friend, Thomas Merton said, "You say you do not think you love God, and that is probably perfectly true. But what matters is that God loves you, isn't it? If we had to rely on *our* love where would we be?"[2] Where indeed?

When we become aware of God's presence, it is good to acknowledge our complete dependence on his love, grace, and mercy. This isn't bad news for our souls. It's the greatest news there is. There were times in my journey when I imagined that my love for God was profound. (What an embarrassing sentence to write.) I thought there was much evidence of just how much greater my love for God was than most others'. What a silly, prideful perspective. Now I feel more like Merton's friend. Where in the world would I be if everything depended on my faithful love for God? Nowhere good, I can tell you. That's not what matters most. What matters is that God loves me, right? And it will always matter most.

Jane de Chantal offers a very gracious bit of counsel to us when we realize our weakness and are perhaps a bit overwhelmed with fear or insecurity.

No matter what happens, be gentle and patient with yourself. Once in a while, if you feel particularly weak, without courage, without confidence, force yourself to make affirmations which are the opposite of your feelings. Say with conviction: "My Savior, my All, despite my feelings of misery and distrust, I place all my confidence in You; You are strength for the weak, refuge for the miserable, wealth for the poor; You are indeed my Savior who has always loved sinners." But, dearest, say these or similar words resolutely, without self-pity or tears; then turn your attention to something else.[3]

I've found it easy to be more harsh with myself than gentle, more impatient with myself than patient. This is not the peaceful way of love. I've often treated my own shortcomings and offenses with less mercy or grace than I would those of a friend. It might help if I treated myself in the same way that God does—delighting to be merciful and longing to be gracious. This often means going against negative feelings. As Jane counsels, I can affirm to myself something that counters my unhelpful attitudes. It sometimes helps me to do this aloud (or under my breath if I'm in a public setting). My true self can speak up in keeping with truth when my emotions are being moved by something untrue.

I've imagined myself as a relatively unemotional person. But it would be truer to say that I've often been a person who denies feelings, hides feelings, avoids feelings—at least unpleasant ones. When I do this, they tend to cause me more trouble from their place of hiding than they would out in the light of God's presence. I've been learning to bring that which I think and feel out into God's merciful, kind, and gracious light and then decide how I'd like to proceed. When I avoid my anxious feelings, they tend to overrun my life. When I notice my feelings and find good ways to express them (or redirect them), it's more likely that my true self, created in the image of Christ, leads me.

One of the great challenges (and therefore opportunities) is to learn to notice the voice of anxiety with a bit of holy objectivity. Rather than presuming that the impulse of anxiety is my only option, I can learn to recognize it as a familiar, if often mistaken, voice in my life.

One practical way I do this is to imagine that unhelpful feelings like anxiety, insecurity, or fear are like a young version of myself who feels threatened or intimidated. I find myself imagining that the current, adult, me can speak with gentle, gracious words to that anxious little one or panicky teen within me, to comfort and encourage him. I express care to him that perhaps he doesn't feel otherwise. I speak to him what God is saying to me in the present moment—words of kindness and care. I'm not speaking wishful words but true ones. Truth like that is so good for my soul. It's a way of acknowledging the reality of my real dependence on God.

In this journey of loving abandonment to God's loving presence with us in each moment, pleasant or unpleasant, welcome or unwelcome, we can take to heart the counsel of David Benner. He suggests that we're tempted to pursue "a spirituality of success and ascent, not a spirituality of failure and descent. We want a spirituality of improvement, not a spirituality of transformation. But the way of the cross is the way of descent, abandon and death. This is the foolishness of the gospel."[4]

Benner highlights the dynamics of the cross as descent, perhaps even apparent failure. The cross does not improve what already is. It transforms us into something and someone we couldn't have imagined possible. An electric chair does not conjure any positive images; it is death for a criminal. The cross was the same sort of image in the first century. But it was transformed into an image of transformation and freedom that comes through loving abandonment to God's purpose in the present moment.

One of the practical ways to keep the reality of the cross before us has come from the monastic tradition. I've heard it whenever I've joined a monastic community in their night prayers. At the close of communal prayers at the end of a day, the monks pray for the grace of a quiet night and a good death.

The Rule of Benedict says it this way: "Day by day remind yourself that you are going to die."[5] One of the desert fathers suggested that a key facet of the watchfulness that we are to cultivate in our lives is always "to have the thought of death in one's mind."[6] In our day, we are less likely to be obsessed with death than to avoid the thought of our eventual death. But the monastic tradition recommends neither. Just remember that you will not live in this body on this earth forever.

Like everyone, we will eventually die. I will live forever as an eternal being made in the image of God, but this chapter of my life will not last forever. Someday, I will likely attend a memorial service for my parents. Someday, my three sons may well attend a memorial service for their mom and their dad. This isn't morbid. It is an opportunity to receive the present moment as it is: precious and fleeting. Time is too short to treat ourselves or others with harshness, impatience, or unkindness. There is a simple, humble, trusting way to live that leads to peace.

STEWARDSHIP OR OWNERSHIP

When it comes to engaging in the life and work God has entrusted to us, we tend to think in terms of "ownership" when God tends to communicate in terms of "stewardship." This is another facet of the dependence and surrender to which we're invited. For example, Paul speaks of the work to which God called him like this: "This is how one should regard us, as servants of Christ and stewards of the mysteries of God. Moreover, it is required of stewards that they be found faithful" (1 Corinthians 4:1-2 ESV).

Imagining myself as *owner* of my own life may sound empowering, but it may be a kind of independence that makes life and work heavier. Seeing myself as a *steward* of my life is actually freeing and empowering. I'm part of something bigger than my own ideas, my own strategies, my own efforts. Believing that everything in my life will rise and fall only on my efforts fails to take into account that I have been invited to become a servant of a kingdom that is beautiful, inspiring, empowering. I am following the One who is truly Owner. A vision of my life as an ownership to manage has a way of provoking my anxieties; entering into my life as a stewardship entrusted to me by a generous, gracious God feels like a well-fitting yoke.

One morning, Gem and I were sitting in my downstairs home office, complaining to each other about how uninspired we were feeling about our work of writing. We were both working on book projects and were struggling. As we were having that conversation, I looked out the sliding glass door and noticed that there were a few doves congregated on our back lawn and back fence. We've often felt like the sighting of a dove is God affirming his delight in and tender care for us as his trusting children. There was a season when I felt that God's special name for me was "my little dove."

As we looked at those doves on our lawn, more doves came and landed on our patio cover, the back fence, and the lawn. Eventually, there were fifteen doves in view. Having lived in this house for twenty-five years, we've never seen that many doves at one time in our yard. We both felt overwhelmed and grateful.

I asked Gem, "If this were a message from God, what would that message be?" Gem suggested, "You have more than you need. I will care for you." I asked aloud if any of the doves looked worried about getting breakfast, let alone about writing a book. None of them did. We both felt a surge of encouragement and energy, and returned with hope to our creative work. We were able to re-engage our work from the holy energy of peace.

UNION WITH PEACE

There is a way of finding ourselves at home on the path of peace. That way is in trying on and putting into practice the good counsel of our God. God's counsel leads us to places of peace if we'll trust him and follow him. James puts it this way:

> Do not merely listen to the word, and so deceive yourselves. Do what it says. Anyone who listens to the word but does not do what it says is like someone who looks at his face in a mirror and, after looking at himself, goes away and immediately forgets what he looks like. But whoever looks intently into the perfect law that gives freedom, and continues in it—not forgetting what they have heard, but doing it—they will be blessed in what they do. (James 1:22-25)

James tells us that we haven't gone far enough when we simply listen to a good word. Knowing the way of peace is not the same as walking in the way of peace. I can read a wise book or hear a good message, but then walk away having only tasted it rather than intending to practice it. It is in good practice that we find peace. James suggests that when we stop at hearing, we're like the person who gets up in the morning, sees in the mirror that he has a day's worth of beard and disheveled hair, feels good that he noticed it, but then does nothing to address what he's seen.

I love teaching. I seek to share good things with those I teach. I've learned that it helps if I find ways to give time for those who listen to imagine what it would look like to live the insights I share. If I pour on the teaching without much space for reflection and holy imagination for listeners to put what they learn into practice, I'm training people to become comfortable with a great deal of undigested, unpracticed knowledge. I'm sure that's not what any teacher intends.

But we can end up training people to do what James says we shouldn't—listen to the Scriptures without acting on what they hear. The sheer quantity of information we provide can make it far less likely that listeners will know what to do next, let alone have time to do it. The *how* of our teaching has trained them more than the *what* of our teaching. And that much unaddressed insight can provoke a dull anxiety in our souls. We intuitively recognize that there is a good way that we know about but are not growing in.

I've found the Scriptures full of wisdom for living and working well. I've best experienced that wisdom shaping and guiding me when I experiment with what I'm learning. In this way, I find my way to the freedom James mentions. Practice helps us learn how truth works. It highlights what it is in us that makes it hard to live well.

Dependence and surrender aren't popular invitations. But they are tested pathways to grow in peace of soul and peace in community.

NON-ANXIOUS REFLECTION

- What do you feel when you hear these words: *dependence* and *surrender*? What resistance arises in you? Is there anything that feels inviting in them? This could be a very fruitful conversation to have with the God who invites you into these postures.

- Have you ever found yourself offering a great sacrifice to avoid a simple obedience? How did this make you feel? What fruit did that sacrifice produce? What might have been the outcome of doing what God was actually inviting you to do?

- Are there times when you find yourself more focused on how much you love God (or don't love God) rather than beginning with how much God loves you? Where does this tend to lead your soul?

8

A BUOYANT LIFE

I wish it weren't true, but an anxious life has felt like the normal path for too long. What I'm glad for is that God has been helping me learn a more buoyant posture than anxiety. I've discovered that joy can bring strength to my soul when anxiety has drained me. Hope has encouraged me about my future with God when anxiety continues to make dire predictions about the path ahead. And contentment, that very un-American virtue, has been a place of learning that my life is already a good one, when anxiety would sour my present and my future with its scarcity thinking.

Joy, hope, and contentment have not come easily to me. I often find myself gravitating toward heaviness, hopelessness, and dissatisfaction. These good soul postures have required spiritual training. I've needed to learn from Jesus how to become at home in them when I've been surrounded by their opposites for so long. It doesn't work to *try* to be more joyful or hopeful or content. But I have been learning how to be in training to grow strong in these holy postures of soul.

A JOYFUL GOD

As I've had opportunity to share what I've been learning about the unhurried and peaceful ways of God-with-us, I will often hear myself say something that *I* need. That shouldn't be any surprise. Why wouldn't the Wonderful Counselor who offers his counsel *through* me speak *to* me at the same time? When I share with others counsel that I deeply believe for them, I can also take it to heart myself. This isn't a moment for self-accusation or self-condemnation. It is an invitation to humble self-awareness and receptivity.

One of the delights of my ministry was an extended season of biweekly Zoom meetings with key leaders from nations across Africa. In one of those video conversations with African leaders, I found myself sharing a line that Dallas Willard said more than once: "There is no more joyful being in the universe than God."[1] I realized that it seemed easier to believe on behalf of others than for myself. Envisioning God's joy toward me and in me feels unfamiliar. I don't recall persons of authority in my early life as being particularly joyful. But God *is*. In this present moment of my life, God finds joy in me. God does not find it difficult to smile at me. God enjoys my fellowship. Over time, the reality of God's joy is becoming infused into my assumptions, expectations, and perspectives. And joy lightens my anxious heart and mind.

How am I learning to live this way more? Maybe it sounds simplistic, but it has helped when I make this a matter of simple prayer. I ask that the Spirit of Joy would teach me joy. Who better to teach me? I then find myself watching for evidence of God's joy in me or around me. I lean on the mercy of God to make me more at home in the joy of Father and Son in the Spirit.

I simply ask for God's help because I have too often limited my own access to his joy. I have struggled to imagine myself surrounded by a joy that is rooted in peace. I need God's help to enter into a joy that doesn't come easily to me. I can ask for this lightness of God's Spirit to be more present to me than my anxieties are.

This is something Jesus is already working at even before I ask. His joy is present for me to simply receive moment by moment. Even my desire for God's joy is an outward expression of God's inward work. God the Father and God the Son want their joy to fill me. My praying isn't about convincing God of something, but about receiving what God is already longing to give.

This is something to remember when my anxiety feels like carrying a heavy weight in my soul. It pulls down the joy that the Spirit would cause to rise from within me. Why am I carrying this weight? I could find a way to set it down if I wished. What will I do with my heavy, anxious thoughts? How will I make my way into life-giving joy? How will I make my way under my negative surface moods so that I can engage my life and my work well?

It sometimes helps when I pivot my attention from these heavy moods to contemplate the real presence of God-with-me in Christ. Christ is truly a Prince of Peace. The Spirit of Christ is the Spirit of Joy. This is fruit he bears in my life, if I'll let him. Christ wants his own joy to fill my mind and heart (John 15:11).

I sometimes find myself in seasons that don't feel very peaceful or joyful. Often situations arise that provoke my anxiety in deeper and more profound ways than usual. And the messages that come with these challenging circumstances don't help: "You're trapped. You're doomed. There is no hope. Nothing will ever change." Who is speaking words like that to me? They certainly don't sound like the voice of a Prince of Peace, a God of hope, a Savior who longs that his joy would fill me as it does him.

Peace and joy are well-suited to one another. They are good friends. Peace is a deep well from which joy can bubble up. And joy has with it a more peaceful tone than outward excitement does. Joy like this isn't mostly an ecstatic response to things going the way I prefer. Joy is holy energy and buoyancy that rises from my depths where Christ is at home by the Spirit. Every day, this gift of God's own peace and joy are present to me—in me.

As I write these words, I hear the strong Santa Ana winds blow outside. They bring the heat of the desert to our coastal climate. They have a way of clearing the air even as they heat it. Wouldn't it be good if I experienced the strength of God's Spirit blowing through my heart and mind to clear away depression and anxiety? I sense the beginnings of a holy breeze even as I write these words. I hope you sense the same as you read them. May it grow into a strong wind that refreshes our inner life.

GIVING HOPE, FINDING HOPE

Another buoyant dynamic that pairs well with peace is *hope*. Anxiety flourishes in places of despair. I've especially found help here in the words of blessing I find throughout the Bible. I see them as words that give us what they talk about. Among my favorite verses of blessing are these words of Paul to his friends in Rome: "May the God of hope fill you with all joy and peace as you trust in him, so that you may overflow with hope by the power of the Holy Spirit" (Romans 15:13).

When Paul writes words like these, he expects that something real will happen in the lives of those he blesses. What might have been Paul's intention for the Romans as he wrote these words of blessing? What did he envision happening in their lives?

First, he wanted them to see God as the God of hope in circumstances that likely felt hopeless to them. They lived in the capital city of the Roman Empire. It wasn't a place that was very hospitable to those who had decided to become followers of Jesus, a Jewish Messiah, and to a faith foreign to Roman religion. In a world where the future would likely hold persecution and suffering for them, they had put their faith in a God of hope. Where they might understandably worry about a hard future, they could find hope for their future in God.

This solid hope in the person of God revealed in Christ would enable them to find great joy and deep peace as their confidence in God grew. They might come to see themselves surrounded by everything they needed to live in fullness and well-being. They would be able to count on God's goodness even when they might anticipate badness in the world around them.

Paul envisioned that this confident perspective would bear a generous harvest of hope in their lives. God's Spirit would bear that fruit mightily in and through them. They would become people who brought a hopeful posture to hopeless circumstances. Their hope was not in things going as they wished, but in the God who would be with them no matter what happened.

We need this sort of hopeful perspective when anxieties seek to overwhelm us. When we look around us and see little reason to hope for a good future, we can find reliable hope in the God of hope. This is a blessing we can count on and grow to trust more and more.

THE ROLE OF WISDOM

It has helped me to connect the buoyant life of joy and hope with the God-given gift of *wisdom*. I need to see things as they are, and God helps me. In his letter, James suggests that "if any of you lacks wisdom, you should ask God, who gives generously to all without finding fault, and it will be given to you" (James 1:5). Here is a prayer God always enjoys answering: a request for wisdom. Wisdom is gained in the challenges we face (the "many trials" of verse 2), when we live those trying times in the presence of God. Wisdom is lived knowledge. Wisdom is knowing how truth actually works. Wisdom is what we need in our very anxious world. Insight is seeing into how things really are in light of God-with-us. This is where hope and joy grow.

If we admit to God that we don't know how to proceed or that we don't understand something, he does not find fault with us. He does not look down on us. He is generous with wisdom.

James goes on to remind us that "when you ask, you must believe and not doubt, because the one who doubts is like a wave of the sea, blown and tossed by the wind. That person should not expect to receive anything from the Lord. Such a person is double-minded and unstable in all they do" (James 1:6-8). James's comments about doubt, when I first heard pastors teach about it, always sounded shaming, like a negative assessment of our failures of faith. It is, instead, simply a statement of fact and a word of wisdom James is passing along. You cannot turn both left and right in the same moment. You cannot travel both forward and backward at the same time. You cannot drive both north and south concurrently.

James seems to be saying, "Have hopeful confidence in God. Trust deeply that God really is generous and kind. God does not condemn us when we admit our lack of knowledge or insight in a particular situation. He knows our weakness, and he is the sort of loving Father who wants his daughters and sons to do well."

When we live without confidence in God's goodness and care, we are like waves in a sea being blown wherever the wind takes them. As James says, this sort of doubt about the good, beautiful, and true nature of God makes us unstable and conflicted. We become anxious. We can't live and move with confidence because we really aren't sure in which direction to go.

One piece of wisdom that has been proving especially good for me is what Jesus says to his inner circle on their last night together. "Do not let your hearts be troubled. You believe in God; believe also in me" (John 14:1). The way Jesus says this suggests that I can learn how to have an untroubled heart in a troubling situation.

Apparently, I am not trapped by my troubles. Hardships do not necessarily have to soak into my heart. Jesus is willing to teach me to trust rather than to be troubled in heart. Just realizing that this is a *possibility* has often made a great difference for me. The vision Jesus offers to untrouble my heart in troubling times sounds like this: "My Father's house has many rooms; if that were not so, would I have told you that I am going there to prepare a place for you? And if I go and prepare a place for you, I will come back and take you to be with me that you also may be where I am" (John 14:2-3).

I have a home in God. There is plenty of room in the Father's house for me. It's already mine even if it isn't obvious now. If I believe in God, I can trust what Jesus is saying here.

Being at home in God is the place from which I really can live and work, no matter what is happening around me. This isn't a denial of reality. It's an affirmation of reality. A mood or a passing feeling is not my deepest reality. It's more like a morning marine layer that burns off as the day arrives in its fullness. It may feel like there is no sun, but it is there, just above the fog. The sun is actually what is burning the fog away. I don't have to let the fog of my mood determine the perspective of my soul.

This is still challenging for me. A heavy mood at the beginning of the day sometimes never seems to burn away. The fog feels more real to me than the sun does. And the fog sometimes tempts me to close my eyes so that when the sun arrives, I don't see it. I assume the fog is still there. I let my vision get fogged in. I let this fog into my soul. I let it dull me, discourage me, weigh me down.

What Jesus seems to be teaching me is to keep looking to him in troubling situations. He is always with me. Always. I have never been alone even when I have felt alone. Jesus is at work. Jesus is hopeful where I'm tempted to lose hope. He is joyful when my soul is heavy. He is the Prince of Peace when I feel anxious.

ENCOURAGING MYSELF

Sometimes, even with this wisdom in mind, negative thoughts still have a way of burdening me. They feel overwhelming. I find help in the Psalms when I realize this is happening.

> Why, my soul, are you downcast?
>> Why so disturbed within me?
> Put your hope in God,
>> for I will yet praise him,
>>> my Savior and my God. (Psalm 43:5)

Why indeed. Sometimes my soul feels heavy or troubled. Why is that? What am I focusing on that is troubling my soul? What am I carrying that is weighing down my soul? There is a way of lifting my eyes to God, my Savior, watching for God's goodness and seeking to find hope in God rather than becoming anxious about the hopelessness that surrounds me. I can speak to that troubled, weighed-down part of me and ask him to look to the God of hope and rescue.

It's what Jeremiah does when he sits and looks out over the smoldering ruins of Jerusalem. He must have felt his ministry was a failure. In Lamentations, he shares his thoughts.

I remember my affliction and my wandering,
the bitterness and the gall.
I well remember them,
and my soul is downcast within me.
(Lamentations 3:19-20)

When Jeremiah's thoughts are filled with what troubles him, what has distracted him, what tastes bitter in his situation, his soul is also downcast. When these are the thoughts he rehearses, he becomes anxious and depressed.

But without denying the reality of the hard place in which he finds himself, he turns his thoughts in a different direction.

Yet this I call to mind
and therefore I have hope:
Because of the LORD's great love we are not consumed,
for his compassions never fail.
They are new every morning;
great is your faithfulness. (Lamentations 3:21-23)

Jeremiah finds hope as he recalls his real experiences of God's great love, God's deep compassion, God's fresh care, God's great faithfulness. He remembers the real goodness of God that he has experienced, and he does this right in the face of the very real bitterness of his present situation. In this way he finds hope. He comes to trust that there is still good in his present even if he is struggling to see it. He grows confident in the goodness that is coming his way. And Jeremiah determines to wait with trust on the goodness of God coming into his life.

When it feels like anxiety will absolutely consume me, I recall that God's great love won't let this happen. The anxieties that filled my mind and heart five years ago are hard to remember now. What I worried about as I imagined a terrifyingly bad future rarely happened. This isn't to say that I always understand what God is doing at any given moment. Maybe God is working in ways I cannot see, because I keep looking for ways *I* want him to work but I am not seeing them.

SOUL ABUNDANCE

Along with the soul posture of joy and hope, I've discovered help in cultivating the goodness of *contentment*. While we often contrast contentment with greed, I've found that it is also a contrast to anxious scarcity.

Contentment isn't a very popular virtue in our Western culture. That's an understatement, isn't it? Contentment sounds like admitting defeat in the race for the good life. It sounds like settling when you could be chasing down more goodness. But true contentment is an invitation to inner well-being regardless of outward circumstance. It doesn't require an ideal and preferred situation to flourish. It realizes that the fullness that matters most is both hidden and eternal.

Consider Paul's confident statement: "I have learned to be content whatever the circumstances. I know what it is to be in need, and I know what it is to have plenty. I have learned the secret of being content in any and every situation, whether well fed or hungry, whether living in plenty or in want. I can do all this through him who gives me strength" (Philippians 4:11-13).

Contentment isn't automatic. Discontentment seems a far easier posture to take, like coasting downhill in a car in neutral.

Contentment is something we learn like Paul did. Paul's satisfaction in communion with God had been tested by both need and plenty. In need, the temptation is to think that our lacks define our lives. But experiences of lack can show us that when we don't have something we need, we still have God. That's not merely an inspiring greeting card sentiment. It's a statement of eternal reality. It is life-giving wisdom. Contentment is an awakening to what we already have when we don't feel we have enough of something.

But circumstances of plenty test us as well. When we have many good things (too many?), we are tempted to think that they define the goodness of our lives. Jesus says that our lives do *not* consist in the abundance of our possessions, but our culture disagrees. Most marketing messengers promise that if we add their product to our collection, our lives will radically improve. Their strategy for our lives is to keep us discontent to ensure their job security.

Paul tells his friends in Philippi that he had learned the *secret* of contentment. I wonder how many of us have learned that secret. I've been slow to learn it. It is the secret of finding satisfaction and joy somewhere other than in an ideal life situation. I can learn contentment in communion with Christ who strengthens me for this good perspective. Contentment is enjoying what I have in Christ in the midst of whatever little or much I possess in this world.

We need strength to live well in seasons of being well cared for and in plenty. In North American contexts, we assume that this is the easy side of the continuum, but it just might be a more challenging trial. Having lots of cash or material goods does not give us life. A new thing in the mail from Amazon does not bring life with it. Jesus gives life to those who have plenty who trust in him, just as he does those who are poor who trust in him. Believing that external goods are the source of life is the poverty of the wealthy. Anxiety and striving are the toxic emissions of discontentment. Peace is the fruit of contentment that grows in the holy experience of communion with God. Sadly, discontentment and anxiety are familiar neighbors.

My anxious discontentment has been the fruit of clinging to a distorted image of God as a miser. Who wouldn't worry if they believed that God was in the habit of withholding what is necessary for a good life? When I've held on to such misguided assumptions about God's posture and perspective on my life, it has cost me. I've grown anxious, hopeless, discouraged, and lethargic. So one of the ways I've come to be less anxious is by coming to rely more and more on the vision of God I see in the face of Christ.

Contentment discovers fullness in the fullness of God. Anxious discontentment is constantly searching for a good life somewhere out on the horizon. The secret of contentment is that fullness is already here because God is already here. My life is not somewhere else. It is here and now in the God of grace, the God of generosity, the God of joy.

What a gift to learn from the Prince of Peace himself to embrace his joy in us, to find hope in his faithful presence, and to rest in contentment in the very blessed life I have already been given.

NON-ANXIOUS REFLECTION

- Have you had experiences of Jesus as joyful toward you? What would or does it feel like to have his own joy filling your perspective and posture? Ask God for help in growing in the buoyancy of joy.

- When you think about the future, do you feel more hopeful or more hopeless? In what ways are you envisioning hard circumstances in your future, whether those are likely or unlikely? How might imagining the presence of God-with-you, no matter what happens in the future, breathe hope into your soul?

- How do you feel about contentment? In what way does it feel inviting? In what way does it seem unrealistic? How might a vision of God's fullness in you affect your sense of internal contentment?

9

CONFRONTING THE GIANT

I've sometimes felt like my struggle with anxiety is like confronting Goliath. I've wanted to learn how to see my Goliath through the eyes of faith and courage that David had in his confrontation with the real Goliath. David's vision of Goliath, as compared to the vision of Saul and the rest of Israel, has been teaching me how to face my own struggle with anxiety.

CONFRONTING GOLIATH

In the David and Goliath story, Goliath had been coming out day after day, for forty days, to make his taunts and threats at the people of God. He thought their dependence on a god was weakness and foolishness. David thought otherwise. Their very different visions of God would soon be put to the test.

David arrived as these two great armies were in a great standoff. The story tells us that Saul and all of the people of Israel there were dismayed and terrified at the Philistine's threatening words. Eugene Peterson suggests that their fear is evidence that they had a Goliath-dominated imagination.[1] They are the favored people of God, but that vision was superseded by a vision of being threatened by a giant of a man named Goliath. The horizon of their attention was filled with a vision of what would happen if (when) the Philistines won. It was a fearful, disheartening, anxious vision. I empathize.

Anxiety has often been my Goliath. It's been helpful to ask myself what have been some of the Goliaths that have terrorized me, disheartened me, discouraged me, and drained me of energy, initiative, and holy activity. How is anxiety intimidating me, threatening me, overwhelming me?

Sometimes my Goliath was an apparently threatening situation. At others it was a daunting project that seemed beyond my capacity. At still other times, it was a challenging relationship or a deep wound. It might have even been an overwhelming temptation.

Peterson calls the condition of the Israelite army "Goliath-sickness." Their imaginations, their perspectives, their motivations were completely overcome by a vision of Goliath as overwhelming. Perhaps you have been Goliath-sick at one time or another. I clearly have. Peterson reminds us that "the moment we permit evil to control our imaginations, dictate the way we think, and shape our responses, we at the same time become incapable of seeing the good and the true and the beautiful."[2]

But into this scene came David. He saw the exact same scene with very different eyes. His was a God-saturated imagination. He had grown up watching for how God would be with him. He had come to experience the trustworthy presence of God in his real life, and now trusted that God with the challenges of the present.

We have so many beautiful David prayers in our Scriptures. They help us see how David cultivated his God-saturated life. For instance, Psalm 16 speaks to whatever Goliath-like scenarios you find yourself in these days.

> I say to the LORD, "You are my LORD;
> apart from you I have no good thing."

I say of the holy people who are in the land,
   "They are the noble ones in whom is all my delight."
LORD, you alone are my portion and my cup;
   you make my lot secure. (Psalm 16:2-3, 5)

What a beautifully God-drenched prayer! Prayers like these can soak our imaginations with the reality of God-with-us. David, with this vision of God-with-him, expected to have as much success with this giant Philistine as he had with the lion and the bear who attacked his flocks in his youth. In terms of my journey with anxiety, I have been helped as my imagination has slowly changed from being Goliath-dominated to being more God-drenched.

Back to our David and Goliath story. Saul's imagination, being Goliath-dominated, was certain that David stood no chance. He didn't see how God was with them. And so, ironically, the help he offered David was really help on Goliath's terms. It's what happens when our imaginations, our thoughts, our perspectives become Goliath-dominated. We rearrange and manage and conduct our lives as though Goliath were god. But anxiety doesn't determine the terms on which we engage our battle. God does.

But David didn't welcome Saul's help. He refused Saul's misguided assistance. David didn't come seeking Saul's help. David already knew he had God's help, and so he knelt down to pick up his five smooth stones.

A while back, Gem and I were given the gift of two weeks in Israel. On one of those days, our bus pulled to the side of a highway southwest of Jerusalem. We were visiting the traditional site of this David and Goliath story. While there, I picked up a small, smooth stone in the dry creek bed where tradition has it that the

David and Goliath confrontation happened. (I'm pretty sure I didn't actually find one of David's five stones.)

I once found that stone again and put it on my writing table. Every once in a while, I'd pick it up and hold onto it as I tackled certain challenging tasks before me. It helped me rekindle my own God-drenched imagination as I faced my own Goliath-like anxiety.

Like David, one of the ways that I've been able to cultivate this God-drenched vision of my life and my work has been through the liturgy of worship in community. Liturgy, over time, makes our hearts a bit more God-shaped. It reflects more and more of God's light into our minds, and it saturates our imaginations with a truer, better, and more beautiful vision of God-with-us.

PEACE WITH OUR CARING SHEPHERD

Another biblical image that has helped me when I feel threatened by my own Goliaths is God as our good shepherd. I find this a caring, peaceful image. Listen to the encouragement of Isaiah.

> He tends his flock like a shepherd:
>> He gathers the lambs in his arms
> and carries them close to his heart;
>> he gently leads those that have young. (Isaiah 40:11)

The shepherding of God is not utilitarian. He is not a self-serving sheep farmer who provides just enough care until the time for slaughter arrives. The Lord is a *shepherd*. Isaiah describes shepherd-like care as personal and tender. A good shepherd carries lambs very close to his heart. God carries us close to his heart. He leads us gently, not harshly. Can you see how this vision and experience of God would deepen our sense of peace and hope in his presence?

In my long struggle with anxiety, one thing that has made a great deal of difference is whether I felt hopeful or hopeless about the possibility of change. Too many times, I concluded that "I'm just an anxious person," as though anxiety were an unchanging element of my God-given identity. What a silly and unhelpful thing to cling to as a core belief. It became a kind of stronghold in my life, preventing me from entering onto a pathway of change. Peace as a stable way to live came to feel impossible for me. So *hope* was an important component of my beginning to enter into change.

In chapter eight, I shared one of my favorite blessings of Paul in his letters (Romans 15:13). I love how it turns out in the Message version: "Oh! May the God of green hope fill you up with joy, fill you up with peace, so that your believing lives, filled with the life-giving energy of the Holy Spirit, will brim over with hope!"

It makes a difference when I learn to see in God the goodness that I long for in myself. This is the contemplative engine of learning to live a more non-anxious life. For some time now, it has been especially helpful and important for me to recognize the presence of the Prince of Peace in my life.

ANXIETY ALONG THE WAY

One of the particular ways that anxiety proves a Goliath presence is the way it seeks to discredit the power and presence of God in my life. I have had a bad habit of allowing anxiety too much credibility to how it predicts dire futures. These pessimistic visions of disasters that loom on my horizon have rarely been realized. But until I observe this habit at work, I invest a great deal of emotional energy forecasting the terrible cost of those potential futures.

Once, when I was traveling from Los Angeles to Newark, New Jersey, on my way to Russia, my flight had to return to the gate because the pilot had an indicator light saying one of the doors was not fully closed. In the end, the flight left one hour late. And I had exactly a one-hour layover in Newark.

I did the mental math and decided I was, inevitably, going to miss my next flight and was going to have to find another way to St. Petersburg, Russia. Anxiety was prophesying doom on my horizon. Every option I could see had me arriving a day later. So I worried about how that would affect my schedule there. I worried about how to get word to my contact there about the delay.

What actually happened? On the way to Newark, the pilot managed to make up fifteen minutes of time due to a favorable jet stream pushing us along. The airline was aware of my narrow connection and had already planned to hold the flight for me. I was able to jog from my arrival gate to my departure gate in just five minutes. When I arrived, the agent saw my name and she said to her partner, "We've got our Los Angeles passenger. We can close the doors now." And, somehow, they managed to get my luggage directly over, so it arrived in time as well. In the end, I arrived at St. Petersburg at exactly the time I was scheduled to.

So, the emotional energy and mental focus I spent thinking through the bad news scenarios was utterly wasted energy. If in fact I had arrived too late for my next flight, the airline would have been responsible to find me another way there. They would have found me another flight, and likely given me a place to stay overnight if it was a next-day departure. I had packed a change of clothing in my carry-on luggage, as I usually do, in case of such a surprise. A hotel would have had other necessities I might not have put into my carry-on bag.

So in this scenario, my anxiety truly did nothing to improve my situation. It did not provide me with creative solutions to an unexpected challenge. It did not provide me wisdom for how to make my way forward with the change in my circumstances. And I did not need *any* of my contingency thinking in the end. My itinerary went just as the airline had said it would. I could have chosen peace over anxiety and been just fine.

But my challenge is to believe that everything is going to be well when I'm faced with an unwelcome change. I keep thinking my anxious forecasting of future doom just might be right this time, even though it has been wrong so many times before. In the end, the Lord shepherds me well, and I do not find myself in want.

Anxiety narrows my vision and excludes good options from my tunnel-visioned view. Peace keeps my perspective open, relaxed, wiser, and more creative. I must remember that my anxiety not only gains *nothing* for me, but it has often cost me dearly.

ANXIETY CONSTRICTS

Anxiety often leads me to jump to conclusions with little evidence for them. I become Goliath-reactive. Once I was on an extended retreat on the East Coast when I felt drawn to take a long walk. The retreat center at which I was staying was nestled in a neighborhood of large, expensive homes. As I walked past these impressive structures, I came to a sign on the road that said "Members Only." I was trying to make my way to a lighthouse, which was down the road from this sign. In that moment, I concluded that there was no option for me but to turn around and walk back.

I had intended to walk out on a stone jetty that jutted into a small nearby bay. I had been reading in Isaiah and came to a line that invited me to "shout aloud and sing for joy, people of Zion, for great is the Holy One of Israel among you" (Isaiah 12:6). Since I was on a silent retreat, I assumed that my fellow retreatants might not appreciate my obedience to the psalm in their proximity. Shouting loudly is a great way to worship, but it wasn't the focus of our time away together.

So the next day, I decided I was going to "break the rules" and walk right past that sign. Of course, I quickly came to discover that it was a sign for a driveway off the main road rather than a sign for the public road on which I was walking. My anxiety's interpretation of the sign limited my freedom and hindered me from entering into what I sensed God calling me to do. That happens a lot for me.

I decided to walk to the end of a quarter-mile stone jetty that jutted from the nearby lighthouse. Out there, I would be alone amid the crashing of ocean waves and could shout as loud as I wanted without disturbing anyone's silent retreat. The wind blew strong and the waves crashed loudly against the rocks.

When I got to the end of the jetty, I took a few photos of the nearby coastal town across the bay and the distant Boston city skyline about twenty-five miles away. Then I began to shout. At the top of my lungs, I yelled out words expressing my appreciation for God's greatness. For many minutes, I shouted words of thanksgiving and praise as the wind blew and the waves struck the jetty. It took a bit of shouting to even hear myself, but it felt good and right to use all my energy to brag aloud about God's salvation, God's strength, and God's protection in my life over the years. I tend to be a quiet, soft-spoken person, so this was a good and stretching practice for me. I found confidence to lean into my anxious feelings of timidity rather than being intimidated by them and making premature decisions.

I expressed my praise in the spirit of Isaiah 12—a song about a future day of salvation, a day after they've suffered at the unholy hands of their enemies Philistia, Edom, Moab, Ammon, Egypt, and finally Assyria (Isaiah 11:14-16). It's a song of hearty praise for God's restoring work in their community. The song sounds like one I could have written in seasons that were marked by tangible restoration and abundant salvation—seasons marked more by the fruit of comfort than the work of discipline. Shouting praise to the God who does this work felt right and good.

God is always doing glorious things in our lives and through us in our work. But anxiety has had a way of keeping me from seeing it to celebrate it. I miss enjoying the sweet fruit of such grace. It was never a deserved abundance. It was always given. In such times, my soul seems to speak with a faint whisper rather than with a hearty shout.

Isaiah's song reminds me that God himself is my salvation. God finds a way to finally keep me safe from my enemies (even when I am my *own* enemy). He brings me into places of deep, joyful life. He doesn't just rescue me from what is bad (like he finally does for Israel with Assyria), but he leads me into joyful good (like entering a promised land). His salvation is like a deep and reliable well from which I can draw all the water I need (Isaiah 12:3).

God alone is my strength. God does not give me strength that I can somehow take away on my own apart from his presence. God-*with-me* makes me strong. This strength is the fruit of communion, even union. Anxiety makes me feel weak in the face of a potential threat, but in God I find actual strength to turn and face what worries me.

When I feel weak, God's gracious presence makes me strong. When I feel weary, God's vibrant presence refreshes me. When I am timid or fearful, God is close to me to encourage me. The Lord himself is my strength. My unwelcome feelings don't always change, but their power over me often feels weakened.

AN EXPERIMENT IN HUMAN OMNIPRESENCE

In 2007, an experiment was launched with lots of fanfare.[3] I don't think anyone called it an experiment, but it turns out to have become one. The experiment was the introduction of the iPhone. There were other smartphones introduced before and after it, but it was arguably the most visible and trend-affecting version of this technology. It was, in a way, an experiment in human omnipresence. At any moment, a person could check in on just about anyone or anything in the world.

A few years back, I made an eight-day retreat at the Eastern Point Retreat Center in Gloucester, Massachusetts. Leading up to that retreat I had been on the road more days than I'd been home for many months. It had been a busy season of ministry travel, both domestically and internationally.

So in the first twenty-four hours of retreat, I reflected on my intentions about how to engage, or disengage, from technology, specifically my smartphone. I felt it had become a bit *too* present in my life and I wanted to correct that pattern. It had become a Goliath presence in my life. As I reflected on my plan to set my iPhone aside, I realized how many different roles it had come to play in my life. I was realizing that it was going to take a bit of unraveling to fulfill my intention.

I began to make a list of the various ways I was using my iPhone at that time.

1. It's my watch.

2. It's my alarm clock.

3. It's my library (through ebook apps).

4. It's often my Bible.

5. It's my news source.

6. It's my primary communication center (email, texts, phone calls and Wi-Fi–based app calling).

7. It's how I keep in touch with hundreds of family, friends, and acquaintances (through social media apps).

8. It's a source of entertainment (through YouTube and other web-based content).

9. It's my navigator.

10. It's my travel agent (flights, ride sharing, hotels).

11. It's my camera.

12. It's my stopwatch.

13. It's my financial manager (bank apps, accounting apps).

14. It's my source of music (iTunes and streaming apps).

15. It's my physical trainer (various exercise and fitness apps).

16. It's my weather channel.

17. It's my calendar.

18. It's my address book.

19. It's my task manager.

20. It's my calculator.

21. It's my wallet, more and more.

22. It's my boarding pass for flights.

I bet you can think of other purposes your smartphone serves. Many of those functions used to be served by some other device, item, or person. I used to use a handwritten calendar, a physical address book, a portable cassette tape player, a paper to-do list, and so on. The convenience of my smartphone is that many of those functions can be served in one place. The challenge of my smartphone is that many of those functions require me to remain engaged with my phone more and more of the time.

There are many functions of my smartphone that make life so much easier than it used to be. I'm grateful for those gifts. But while a smartphone is a very powerful servant, it is a tyrannical master. So when I began to feel that my iPhone was becoming too much of a Goliath in my life, I began to search out some of those functions to take back in simpler ways.

So on the second day of my retreat, this list began to come into practical focus. I wrote in my journal,

> I intend to remain unplugged during this retreat as far as my smartphone goes. But what does that mean? I just got back from a walk, but I felt I needed my phone to see where I was going on the map. I found myself then thinking about researching my route back to the airport at the end of the retreat. Would I use ride sharing? Would I get a ride to the train? I could figure that out on the web, but that wouldn't exactly be unplugged. I can easily get lost in this kind of researching, or checking, or simply escaping. I feel an invitation to unplug in as many ways as possible so that I can more fully plug into you, Lord.
>
> How is God with me in all this? Is God angry with me overusing my smartphone compared to what I intended?

Does God want me to add the distance of guilt and shame to the distraction of my device? I hardly think that makes any sense. In any of this, my Father in heaven desires simply that I would draw near to him. He has addressed the issue of guilt and shame in the loving gift of his Son's suffering and death. He is not looking to make me suffer.

Can you identify with my feeling of being attached to my smartphone? It's pretty obvious that it's hard to be on retreat if you're still connected to your phone. I had already decided not to take calls, check messages or emails, or stay connected to social media. But I hadn't thought into all the other ways I use my smartphone in my day. It took that first day for it to dawn on me what phone fasting was going to involve.

When I got home from my retreat, I bought a plug-in digital clock for those days when I need an alarm. As a result, I began to leave my phone charging downstairs in my office at night. My phone was no longer my first engagement of the morning. Instead, I would rise, make myself a cup of home-roasted coffee, then enjoy some time reading Scripture and praying to begin my day. I often engaged a work project next before finally picking up my phone. This has lowered my anxiety and increased my sense of inner peace.

How can you tell if your smartphone is serving you or if you are serving it? One way is to take a break from it for a couple of hours. Pay attention to what happens in you when you don't have it to pick up in a down moment. Notice whether feelings of anxiety arise. You may decide that being that attached to your smartphone is something you'd prefer not to continue.

The dopamine cycle that social media gets us hooked on can be profoundly anxiety producing. In such an addictive situation, will we approach recovery through abstinence, like the alcoholic or drug addict, or in moderation, like the overeater or the workaholic? We may feel that avoiding social media completely would be a bigger liability than benefit, and so choose moderation. The question is whether our relationship with social media is an increasingly anxious one, and whether we want that source of anxiety filling more of our hours and days.

WAITING ON GOD

How might I deepen the sort of God-saturated imagination that I see in David? I've found this helpful from the prophet Isaiah:

> Even youths grow tired and weary,
>   and young men stumble and fall;
> but those who hope in the LORD
>   will renew their strength.
> They will soar on wings like eagles;
>   they will run and not grow weary,
>   they will walk and not be faint. (Isaiah 40:30-31)

The operative invitation is to find hope in the Lord (or to "wait for the Lord"). And the Lord in whom I am invited to hope is loving, gracious, encouraging. A person who has had plenty to teach me about finding hope in God has been David, king of Israel.

I've wondered at times how I would have responded if I were David preparing to confront Goliath. I'm impressed at his confidence. Such confidence does not come as easily to me. I didn't grow up in a church family. I did attend a local Sunday school for a few years in my early childhood. I remember hearing the story of David and Goliath then, but it sounded more like make-believe than a story of truth to my young ears.

Growing up, David had a unique experience of God. As he shepherded the family's flocks, he experienced God-with-him in that work to help him, strengthen him, encourage him, make him hopeful. He experienced God making him strong to confront the bear or the lion that attacked the flock.

David learned to play the lyre and to sing songs praising the God of Israel. He eventually came to write psalms to pour out his heart before this good God. He grew up with a God-drenched imagination. He saw God everywhere. He saw God at work in everything. He had come to trust that God's favor, God's power, God's provision would follow him wherever he went. There was a buoyancy in David's perspective rooted in his confident experience of God. This is how he came to overcome Goliath when the rest of Israel found the giant man intimidating. And this just might be how I learn to overcome the Goliath of my own sometimes overwhelming anxiety.

NON-ANXIOUS REFLECTION

- What in your experience lately has felt like a Goliath? What are some of the Goliath situations in your life that feel burdensome? Can you imagine looking past these realities to the greater reality of your Father in heaven looking to you, coming to you, caring for you?

- Why not take a few moments to think about God as your shepherd? Imagine Jesus with you to guide your steps, care for your life, protect you from lasting harm. Take a few moments to imagine recent situations that were hard, uncomfortable, even painful, and how Jesus was present to you to shepherd you.

- How would you describe your relationship with your smartphone (if you have one)? In what ways is it a gift? In what ways is it a burden, Goliath-like even? Is there any way you feel drawn to change the nature of that relationship?

10

PEACE IN TROUBLING TIMES

God created an Eden-like world for us to live in. It's not very Eden-like today though, is it? There are so many ways in which the world around us isn't nearly as good, beautiful, and true as God intended. There is a lot of human error, human brokenness, and human evil on display. In such a world, peace seems unnatural. We live in a world full of troubles.

Jesus understands troubling times. In the upper room, Jesus spoke words to his inner circle that he knew they would need in the hours to come. They would face the most disorienting, anxious moments of their lives when Jesus was arrested, beaten, crucified, and killed. And so Jesus said to them, "I have told you these things, so that in me you may have peace. In this world you will have trouble. But take heart! I have overcome the world" (John 16:33). What things has he just told them that might help them find peace?

Jesus said what he said so his disciples "will not fall away" (John 16:1). He let them know that his words were meant to help them realize that the world does not know the Father, nor does the world understand Jesus (John 16:3). He told them that there was more he'd like to say to them, but they didn't have the capacity to bear it yet (John 16:12). Mostly in this passage, he was preparing them for the arrest and crucifixion that would soon stun them all.

Now, Jesus reminded them that he spoke to them in a way that would help them find peace in a situation where there would be no peace to be found. This is the genius of Jesus. He does not promise us a life full of easy, happy experiences. He promises his peaceful presence in the real world in which we live. He promises peace to us in conflict and troubles. He promises peace to us when we are opposed or even attacked.

I still have a habit of seeking inner peace out there somewhere: if this problem is solved; if that issue is resolved; if I can figure out what's happening or what's going to happen. But gaining inner peace merely by solving problems out there is tenuous at best. Problems keep coming, and I have a lot less control of problems out there than I think. That's not to say that I don't act for good in the world around me. It's just that if the peace of my soul is based on my success out there, my inner peace is at risk.

We live in a world full of trouble. We need a peace that is more powerful than trouble. It is a mistake to promise people that if they follow Jesus, their lives will be trouble free and full of outward blessings. The peace Jesus promises is better than that because it is durable. It is a peace found *in him*. It is union with Christ that produces settled peace in our hearts and minds. This peace stays when trouble comes. And this peace is something we can bring into the midst of trouble and conflict.

Jesus wants us to realize that it is no surprise when the world brings us trouble. We live in a world that is out of alignment with its divine purpose and origin. There is no peace in opposition to God; it is *in* God that we find peace. Peace like this is like the roots of a tree rather than like the fresh sprouts of spring that fade and wither when summer heat comes.

But when trouble comes, I am often overwhelmed by it. I can agree with the truth of what Jesus says here, but I may find I don't yet have the capacity to trust him as much as I wish. Why do I struggle like this? One reason is that I listen to the wrong voice. When I feel heavy, worried, or overwhelmed, I tend to give attention to the voices fostering these feelings. But these voices aren't usually seeking my good.

The voice of anxiety or overwhelm—when I trust its message— has a way of diminishing me, draining me, and distancing my mind and heart from God's real presence. What helps me is to practice contemplative attentiveness to the voice of God in my life.

God has never forsaken me when I feel forsaken. He has never abandoned me when I feel his apparent absence. God remains a God of peace in moments when anxiety threatens to overwhelm me. I've been learning to attend to God's gracious and peaceful voice in the face of the noisy voice of anxiety. God wants me to let his voice be louder in my heart and mind than the voice of anxiety. In this way, I become more securely connected to the true vine.

But I've sometimes had the habit of responding to unwelcome surprises and painful experiences with a non-abiding rather than an abiding posture. I attach myself to the vine of worry; it sucks life from me. I attach myself to the vine of spiritual apathy; it leads me to procrastinate and put off my life rather than living it. I attach myself to the vine of "What do others think?" and my sense of value rides the roller coaster of others' changing opinions. It's so much better when I learn to practice the habit of abiding in God when I feel uneasy or overwhelmed or frustrated.

Jesus is continually reminding me that he alone is the true vine and that I am a beloved branch. These have become familiar and calming words for me: "If you remain in me and my words remain in you, ask whatever you wish, and it will be done for you. This is to my Father's glory, that you bear much fruit, showing yourselves to be my disciples" (John 15:7-8).

Jesus isn't offering a tricky conditional arrangement here, as though he were saying, "If you abide in me, then I'll let you ask what you wish and I'll do it for you (though only because I'm forced by my own faithfulness to do so)." Jesus is making a simple statement of fact. "If you remain united with me—in communion with me—what you ask and what I want will overlap. The Father will be honored because you are reflecting his heart and mind more, and realizing that in your actual fruitful living."

AT HOME WITH JESUS

Jesus invites us to make ourselves more and more at home with him. My anxiety harbors assumptions about Jesus that don't fit and don't work. When I let anxiety reign, I tend to assume that he has less patience with me than he actually does. Jesus wants us to let him be patient, kind, compassionate, and gentle with us. Jesus wants us to refurnish our vision of him with images that are rich with goodness, beauty, truth, and peace. That's an inviting place to make myself at home.

There is nothing Jesus loves more in friendship with me than that connection. In that place of confident relationship, he is a master to whom I am an apprentice. I'm learning how to live like the Prince of Peace I follow. I'm learning to express his peace in the anxious, angry, and troubling environments in which I sometimes find myself. I need a potent peace to be able to live this way. Such peace overcomes trouble rather than being overwhelmed by it.

Learning to practice peace this way in my inner life involves noticing when unwelcome feelings arise: insecurity, anxiety, apathy, depression, weariness, or despair. I notice them. I acknowledge them. I don't fight with them, but rather I pivot my attention to God-with-me in that moment. I don't pretend I'm not feeling low, edgy, angry, or heart weary.

I learn to turn my gaze toward God in the midst of these real emotions. When I find myself in the sphere of trouble, I remind myself that the sphere of God's gracious and peaceful presence is a far greater one. I am in the presence of One who protects me, secures me, encourages me, refreshes me, energizes me, stirs me. This reality may not immediately change my mood, but a refreshed perspective often enables me to step into whatever good lies before me and engage it with God.

Inner peace is not just a self-serving good. I can bring it into my encounters and interactions with others. Being a peaceful, non-anxious presence to others blesses them.

IS GOD ANGRY?

In my troubles, I'm tempted to believe that the troubles come because God is angry. This provokes great anxiety in me. On an eight-day silent retreat a few years ago, I decided to let Isaiah be my scriptural guide for that week. Reading through the stories of judgment, of exile, and of restoration, I found much that echoed my own experience. In the middle of that retreat, I came to this passage:

In that day—
"Sing about a fruitful vineyard:
    I, the LORD, watch over it;
    I water it continually.

I guard it day and night
  so that no one may harm it.
  I am not angry.
If only there were briers and thorns confronting me!
  I would march against them in battle;
  I would set them all on fire.
Or else let them come to me for refuge;
  let them make peace with me,
  yes, let them make peace with me." (Isaiah 27:2-5)

For Israel, when Isaiah speaks these words, all of this is future—
in *that* day. I heard these words on retreat after a season that had
felt very much like exile. These words sounded like a promise for
the present moment.

They felt like a personal communication from God to me. God
was "Thou" speaking to "me." The line that especially stood out
was "I am not angry." I know I've read that line countless times
before as I've read through the Scriptures many times, but I don't
recall noticing that exact line. A general statement about God as
slow to anger is frequent and familiar. God speaking personally to
his people to say "I am not angry" surprised me.

I heard it especially related to so many ways that I don't
measure up to my own good intentions. I find myself presuming
God views me mostly with disappointment (a mild variety of
anger). So I imagine God at least a little irritated with my failures
to fulfill what I intend toward him. To this, I heard God whispering
through Isaiah 27, "I am not angry. I did not send my son to judge
the world and I am not judging you."

God is not demanding (nor expecting) a perfect performance in my spiritual practices. They are *practices*. As I lean into

them, they are developing something in me—training me in a way of living and working. God is not angry with me. Instead, as Isaiah says, God is watching over my life. He is caring for me like a vineyard owner cares for his own vines. He is guarding me from harm.

What captured my attention even more in Isaiah 27 was how God talked about those who would come against him. If there were briars or thorns confronting him like enemies, he would confront them back or, if they were willing, he'd happily make peace with them and turn them into friends. It is not God's preference or pleasure to treat people with anger.

So when I distract myself because I'm afraid there are unpleasant truths to be faced, God responds with mercy and grace rather than anger and disappointment. God seems to say, "Alan, I want you to hear me: I am not angry. You do foolish things at times. I am not angry. You sometimes fail to live out my love for others. I am not angry with you. I want good for you. I am doing all I can to tend you, nourish you, guide you, bless you. I want the fruit of your life to bless many others. I want this for my glory, not yours. I want to bless you so that you will become a blessing to many, many others. This is what I'm working on. Being angry with you does not further that aim."

SLEEPING IN PEACE

In peace I will lie down and sleep,
> for you alone, LORD,
> make me dwell in safety. (Psalm 4:8)

This line from the Psalms is part of night prayer in the Book of Common Prayer. It has been a meeting place for my soul with

God on countless days just before I retire for the night. David here remembers that the only reason he can lie down at night with a peaceful soul and fall asleep is because God alone is a place to dwell in safety. This can sound like irrelevant poetry to some. There are many perceived dangers in our world; we have all suffered harm in many ways. What does it mean that I can dwell in safety with God and find peace in such a place?

Well, it certainly doesn't mean that as followers of Jesus we will never experience difficult losses or painful wounds. I have faced many over the decades of my life. But even though I bear the soul scars of these losses and wounds, I still find that I can rest in the care of God. This doesn't feel like wearing rose-colored glasses to me. It feels like a description of the state of my soul when I find myself more and more at home in God-with-me, especially when trouble is also with me. God-with-me does not remove pain-with-me or hardship-with-me. Pain still hurts. Loss still stings. But the crucified One empathizes with me in my suffering. Christ has suffered like us, and so he knows and feels our pain.

Anxiety is often what keeps me awake as I lie down to sleep. It is often what wakes me in the middle of the night. I find that directing my attention to God-with-me as I lie in my bed helps me find rest that leads to sleep. God fosters in me a faithful vision of reality so that I can lie down at night, confident that God-with-me enables me to be safe at home in God.

A DIFFERENT VISION OF ANXIETY

My tendency along the way, as it relates to my anxiety, has mainly been to find a way to stop feeling anxious as quickly as possible. I'm looking for quick ways to rid myself of anxious feelings. Anxiety is uncomfortable. It's distracting. It feels counterproductive. But the path by which I act on these feelings makes a great deal of difference. If I seek to simply get rid of anxious thoughts and feelings, I may take the route of avoiding them, trying to run away from my own heart and mind. That's not actually something I can do, because I take myself with me as I try to avoid my own inner realities.

A counselor in my life once said that I needed to learn to take my anxiety with me.[1] If I were to use the metaphor of a vehicle, he didn't recommend that I put my anxiety in the driver's seat. But neither should I try to lock it in the trunk or leave it behind by the side of the road. It is a part of me. Anxiety, at least in some way, might have been an attempt to take care of myself in the best way I knew how. It wasn't the most fruitful strategy, but for a window of time in my young life it was what I had.

In the kingdom of God, I'm realizing that I have more resources than anxiety thought it did. I am safer and more secure in every way that matters, even when bad things happen, than I once thought I was. Taking my anxious thoughts and feelings with me as I grow in this kingdom way of life means letting them sit in the back seat. They aren't driving the car, but they are with me. Maybe, with a little love and compassion, their energy can be turned toward the good life I'm seeking to live and the good work I'm seeking to do.

So it may not be my best strategy to try to get rid of anxiety. It represents energy, God-given but misdirected, that could be recovered and redirected. It could become genuine concern that is pointed toward receiving God's ever-present grace and then sharing it with others along my path. I could learn to practice the real presence in the midst of present anxiety.

When what I am carrying in my work feels heavier than it should or becomes overwhelming, I find myself asking, *What might I have added to the yoke Jesus has entrusted to me that is making it heavier?* Sometimes it is simply my anxiety. Sometimes it is a mindset of obligation rather than joyful desire. Sometimes it is dread instead of hope.

These burden my soul and my body. There is a cumulative heaviness that grows. But there is a lightness and peace that can grow as I learn to discern and live into the yoke of Jesus in my life. It's not that everything becomes a tropical oasis. It's simply that a more peaceful, hopeful, joyful perspective changes how I bear the challenges and responsibilities of my life and work.

This hasn't been an easy journey, but it has been rich and fruitful. Remaining awake and alert to anxiety in me, and learning to bring it with me into the presence of grace and peace has proven to be a path of life. I can trust Jesus to address that in me which is nervous, itchy, unsettled, even frantic. The presence of the God of peace overcomes anxiety.

PEACE IN TURBULENT TIMES

I am writing this book in a restless, anxious time. Peace is hard to find. Profound cultural tensions around political differences are ever-present. Pain and anger from ancient and present racial in-equalities and injustices overwhelm many of us. But I keep re-minding myself that Christ is with us now as he always has been. He remains the Prince of Peace in seasons of conflict, tension, and overwhelm.

There is a peace that Jesus embodies that he then gives to us. It is not a situational peace. It does not require our circumstances to become completely conflict- or trouble-free. Jesus gives us *his* peace. Peace is a facet of his very being, and so in communion with Jesus we find peace in his presence.

Jesus reminded his inner circle in the upper room on the night he would be arrested that he was saying what he said "so that in me you may have peace. In this world you will have trouble. But take heart! I have overcome the world" (John 16:33). As his followers would experience great troubles within hours of Jesus speaking these words, we experience plenty of troubles ourselves— not only general, global troubles, but specific, personal troubles.

Jesus cares about these troubles, but they don't worry him. Jesus is not overwhelmed by anxiety as we have sometimes been. He's been in places like those in which we find ourselves, and worse. He is wiser than we are, mightier than we are, more capable than we are, and more compassionate and caring than we are.

As I learn to take this to heart, I experience the peaceful presence of Jesus with me right in the middle of my very real and present troubles. It is his very own peace that he brings to us by being with us. His peace doesn't require a change in our circumstances. His peace can be with us in any situation. Really. God's great grace brings about deep peace.

There is a difference between the peace that comes when nothing troubling crosses our paths and the peace that is the fruit of communion with the Prince of Peace. Peace the world gives presumes that things are mostly going the way I like, and others are going along with my plans as well. It's a precarious peace. Peace that Jesus gives works in all kinds of situations, many of which seem utterly unfavorable and anxiety-provoking.

PERFECT PEACE IN GOD

In learning to rehearse peace, a few lines from Isaiah have often helped me:

> You will keep in perfect peace
>> those whose minds are steadfast,
>> because they trust in you.
> Trust in the LORD forever,
>> for the LORD, the LORD himself, is the Rock eternal.
>> (Isaiah 26:3-4)

God *wants* to keep us in peace. He *will*, Isaiah says, but how? It happens as our minds—all of the conscious movements within us—increasingly rest rooted in God's trustworthiness. Peace is grounded in a vision of a solid God in a shaky world. Anxiety tends to keep me focused on the shakiness, so that my world feels unstable and unsafe.

In the Hebrew original of Isaiah 26, "perfect peace" is literally "peace, peace." Peace squared. Peace multiplied. A blanket of peace resting on a mattress of peace with a comfortable pillow of peace for good measure. I imagine a loving parent repeating the same comforting word at bedtime to a disturbed little one to calm their fears. "Peace, peace my little one. Peace, peace."

Anxiety wants to discount all this as insipid inspirational language. But Isaiah does not speak in empty rhymes. Isaiah speaks potent poetry. As our trust becomes more rooted and solid, our peace increasingly becomes the norm of our way of living. When I awaken to the fact of my worrying, I can recognize it as an indicator that there is some way in which I might more deeply trust my ever-present, ever-faithful Father in heaven. Rather than feeling bad about my worrying, I can remember that God is speaking words of fatherly comfort and encouragement: "Peace, peace, my son. Peace, peace, my daughter. Trust me. You can, you know."

We are kept in perfect peace when we remain steadfastly in the place of trusting our God who is like an everlasting foundation for our lives. This is what I'm learning. So, again, worry is like a red light on the dashboard of my soul. It awakens me to the opportunity before me to entrust myself to a faithful God rather than trying to manage or control things on my own. The latter is a great temptation and becomes for many of us a deep-rooted habit. But we can learn to trust and entrust instead of worrying and fretting. We really can.

We are living in a day when so many of us long for a greater sense of shared peace among us. Many are drawn to work for peace. What a beautiful and noble intention. What an encouraging and hopeful vision. But how does peace grow in a community? How does that peace touch our world? I'm grateful for the wisdom of Isaiah.

> The LORD's justice will dwell in the desert,
>> his righteousness live in the fertile field.
> The fruit of that righteousness will be peace;
>> its effect will be quietness and confidence forever.
> My people will live in peaceful dwelling places,
>> in secure homes,
>> in undisturbed places of rest. (Isaiah 32:16-18)

Isaiah casts a vision for a time when that which is right will reign. God's justice will be as at home in desolate places as it is in fertile ones. And when what is right reigns—when people come into greater alignment with the heart and purposes of God—there is peace. When the many tune themselves to the One, there is harmony. It's like when all the instruments in an orchestra tune themselves to a single oboe. Because each tunes to the same tone, they are all in tune with one another. And so peace borne of alignment with God makes possible a life in which we resonate with one another. This is what shared peace looks like.

When we try to aim for peace between us one at a time, our differences of perspective are often what meet first. This often leads to conflict and disharmony. Peace is primarily an indirect fruit more than it is a direct pursuit. It is a fruit of God's Spirit reigning in us and among us. And when we, together, seek first God's reign and God's ways, we'll discover our hearts and minds are being drawn together in a union we could never achieve directly. Our shared agreement with God's mind and heart bears the fruit of this beautiful and welcome peace. Together, we can find peace in God even in our troubling times.

NON-ANXIOUS REFLECTION

- How might you feel anxious but choose not to worry about your worries? How might you take your anxiety with you, but in the back seat rather than the driver's seat? How might God help you grow in this wisdom?

- Are there ways in which you fear God might mostly be angry, or at least disappointed, with you? If so, how does it feel for you to hear God saying, "I am not angry with you." Why not sit with that divine word for a while?

- Does anxiety ever keep you awake at night? How might it help to personalize the words of Isaiah 26:3, "God, keep me in profound peace by giving me a clearer vision of your faithful, caring presence with me now"?

11

EMBODIED PEACE

One source of anxiety for me is living too much in my head. It's been important to learn how to live, even pray, in this body God has given me. It's been a gift to learn to live my life more engaged with the physical reality of creation that surrounds me. Giving attention to creation, letting myself engage it with every sense God's given me, has often been a pathway to peace.

I shared earlier that I've taken to heart Jesus' counsel about looking at the birds—literally and often. Whenever the weather permits, I begin my day sitting at my home library desk with the sliding glass door open right in front of me. Every bird I hear sounds happy, joyful, and free. Their songs are more robust as the morning grows. Sometimes, I hear the caw of a crow or the chitter of an oriole. I may hear the song of a mockingbird as its runs through its repertoire, or finches taking advantage of the fresh grape jelly I put out. None of this sounds anxious or fretful.

And in the midst, I can hear the morning commute like a roaring wind underneath it all. And my anxiety is often the continual buzz in my soul. It helps me to pay attention to the sounds of these little ones God has made. They remind me that I am at least as well cared for as they are.

One morning, I rose an hour before sunrise to watch and listen for our neighborhood birds. I appreciate the deep quiet of this hour. It really does help my anxiety when I take Jesus up on his counsel to consider the birds. Now there is nothing but a bit of ambient light rising north of me from the lighted houses down the hill.

I've taken a moment to make myself a cup of hand-roasted Sumatra. What a gift to sip at this mug in the cool, quiet dark of this early morning. I hear a neighbor's car start up below. There is the distant roar of a jet overhead. But not a single birdsong yet. Finally, I hear the chitter of a lone hummingbird somewhere in our eastern hibiscus tree. No sight of it yet. Perhaps I'm hearing hummingbird for "good morning."

Finally, this little one flies across to the western hibiscus. Is she meeting a friend? I hear the lone chirp of perhaps a house finch. I imagine her stretching her wings as she awakes. Now I hear a hummingbird conversation. What mysteries are they sharing? Inwardly, I am calm. The quiet of the morning soaks into my soul. "Awake, my soul! Awake, harp and lyre! I will awaken the dawn" (Psalm 57:8).

Everyone but the hummingbirds seems to be sleeping in. Ah. The raspy chirp of a newcomer. I don't recognize the song. Perhaps, like me, she had a rough night of sleep; yesterday afternoon's coffee stayed with me through the night.

Along with considering the birds, Jesus has invited me also to consider the flowers of the field. I notice the five-petal pink blossoms covering our hibiscus trees. They provide breakfast for my hovering friends. I hear further conversation among their tribe inside those trees.

Sunrise will arrive soon. The twilight of this moment makes everything a bit more visible. The marine layer this morning will prevent me from seeing the sun directly. Perhaps I'll be greeted with a lovely morning glow.

The birds have not yet begun visiting our yard or the feeders I tend. I notice that the seed feeders need to be refilled. I hear the faint chirp of a cricket. He surprises me. Isn't he supposed to take the night shift? A chorus of hummingbirds swells. Are they beginning their dawn awakening hymn?

Sunrise is moments away. More birdsong. Antiphonal twittering in the distance. A mosquito whines at my ear. More birds join the morning chorus. Still none visit our yard or the feeders. They must prefer to move slowly in the morning like I do.

A small community of scaly-breasted munia conspire in the eastern hibiscus. What are they planning? An invasion of our yard for breakfast? Perhaps.

I've been watching and listening for the birds as Jesus invited me. What am I learning? Nothing I've witnessed this morning brings even the faintest sense of anxiety. There has been playfulness. There has been simple presence. Breakfast doesn't yet appear to be a priority, but various expressions of birdsong praise have been on the schedule.

A first munia arrives at the lawn, and then a second. They perch on the low brick wall, waiting for their colleagues. Perhaps it's now time for breakfast. They seem to notice me just a few feet away and aren't as unselfconscious as usual. Yesterday, a whole flock of them landed on the lawn together. They appear to prefer eating in community.

Finally, half a dozen munia have arrived; birdseed is on the menu. I love providing their morning meal. I love being a witness to their community breakfast. Then, in a moment, they swarm away. Unseen danger? Maybe the first signs of a little anxiety? But their song doesn't sound anxious. Caution doesn't have to be anxious. It can be the fruit of wisdom.

A dove flies swiftly by. No time for breakfast yet for this one. Perhaps she'll visit later. Her tribe often eats what falls from the seed feeder, but not now. The cries of the munia fill my ears. They drown the song of the others. Is it antiphonal? Do they sing to one another from hibiscus to hibiscus?

I notice a hawk high and to the west in the neighbor's tree. I wonder if he'll be hunting in our hibiscus as he sometimes does. Perhaps the munia have anticipated him. He has a right to breakfast as much as anyone, but it will cost someone more than just a few seeds. Caution really is in order as the hawk enters the eastern hibiscus and twenty or more munia and other little ones flee in unison. The hawk gives chase and leaves the scene. He doesn't seem to have had success on this food run.

Living a non-anxious life doesn't mean that real danger doesn't sometimes lurk in life. The birds of the air might just become a meal for this predator. But it isn't much of a life to live every moment obsessed with fear of harm, is it?

I notice the hawk return to hide in the eastern hibiscus. I see him through the branches. The smaller birds appear to have wisely vacated their usual home. But the hawk is patient. A finch returns and the hawk sneaks up on it from branch to branch. He draws closer to the finch, and I wonder if breakfast has arrived. The finch finally realizes he's on the menu and flees. The hawk gives chase but comes up empty. All this in an everyday suburban neighborhood.

A few munia return to their hibiscus home. No sign of the hawk's return. Has he been successful in capturing his morning meal? Perhaps. Within moments, our hibiscus appears to be a haven again. My little friends have recovered quickly from being the hunted. Their caution doesn't appear to have led to lasting trauma. Too many past threats and wounds linger as permanent residents in my own soul. But the Lord really is my shepherd, here and now. I really shall not be in want of anything I need.

Unhurried moments to consider the birds enable me to experience peace in my body. Some of the usual embodied symptoms of anxiety have quieted. The peace of God can take up residence in the depths of my somatic self.

ANXIETY AS SURFACE TURBULENCE

This little exercise in paying attention to the birds helps me sink into the goodness of the present moment. My anxieties are like surface turbulence on a lake. If I live my life only at the surface, then those waves toss me around and I'm profoundly unsettled. In that metaphor, my depths are more at peace in the presence of God. Martin Laird, in his book *Into the Silent Land*, describes all our thoughts, sensations, emotions, even inspirations as weather that surrounds us. He says that we are not the weather, but the solid mountain around which the weather shifts and changes.[1]

But anxiety isn't always the result of storms. Sometimes, I feel anxiety in the mundane spaces of life. In days past, great sailing ships would come upon places in the ocean where the wind died for days or weeks on end. These were called the *doldrums*. Technically, it is a band near the equator where northern and southern trade winds end up canceling each other out. Sailors go crazy in the unchanging tedium of the doldrums. The anxiety that is in them rises to the surface.

There are seasons when I don't engage in my usual rhythms of travel and training leaders, domestically or internationally. I return to our library, day after day, to sit at my folding table of a desk. I try to do my work of writing or meeting with people on Zoom. Doldrums. The sameness can make me feel edgy inside. The monotony of schedule and the monochrome of my experience makes me nervous. But places of simplicity like that might be a gift.

SIMPLY ABIDING

One way of understanding our mundane experiences is to think of them as rootedness, of being at home. I've lived in California all my life. We are home to some highly prized wine regions. Napa Valley is perhaps known best, but many other regions have been growing in reputation recently. I've enjoyed many beautiful moments in vineyards over the years. They are lovely places to visit. In the early spring, you can see the beginnings of budbreak that eventually move to flowering and the beginning of fruit. In the summer, the fruit continues to ripen until an early fall harvest. The vines then recover over later fall and winter in preparation for the next season of fruitfulness.

When we look at grapevines, we are likely to notice the beauty of the foliage or especially the abundant fruit in season. But when Jesus talks about grapevines in John 15, he focuses our attention on something particularly mundane: the point at which the branch and the vine meet. Jesus uses the language of *abiding* to describe this connection. With deep and continual connection, the branch will indeed grow green and fruitful. Without that living communion with the vine, the branch can do nothing. That which is mundane is the living connection of the branch in the vine.

My anxiety sometimes looks like me frantically seeking somewhere (or "somewhen") else to be. Anywhere but here and now.

And here and now is the only place that I can abide in the true vine. The only flourishing and fruitful place for me is the present moment lived at home in Jesus. But when someone talks about a vineyard, you never hear stories about the junction of vine and branch. Boring! And yet that is the secret of the blooming and bounty that impresses us in a vineyard. The invitation of our Prince of Peace is to find ourselves quite simply at home in him. That place of simple connection will produce the abundance that will bless our lives and will enable us to do great good for the blessing of others.

So whether we are learning to find peace in the midst of storms, or in seasons that feel more monotone, there is a solid place of peace for us at home with Christ in God.

SPEAKING WORDS OF LIFE

Sometimes, I'll hear a simple phrase of Scripture that captures the essence of living wisdom for me. Recently, I read one of these in the book of Acts in a passage about conflict between the Jewish leaders and the apostles of Jesus. The high priest and his fellow Sadducees were jealous of the public praise of the apostles, so they rounded these first followers up and imprisoned them. The story continues to say that "during the night an angel of the Lord opened the prison doors and brought them out, and said, 'Go and stand in the temple and speak to the people all the words of this Life.' And when they heard this, they entered the temple at daybreak and began to teach" (Acts 5:19-21 ESV).

The apostles are commanded by this angel of the Lord to go to the temple and proclaim to anyone who will listen "all the words of this Life." Jesus is this Life embodied and now risen. There is no proclamation of eternal life apart from living communion with the One Who is Life. This life came to be embodied among us. I don't proclaim a belief system or a religious message. I'm talking about a life I've been learning to live in friendship with Christ.

It is the embodied nature of this life, learning to live into the kingdom in this God-given body, that has been an important element of finding freedom in anxiety. I've lived a lot of my life in my head, in my thoughts, as what James K. A. Smith calls a brain-on-a-stick.[2] This oddly disembodied way of living has had a way of increasing my physical sensations of anxiety.

I've been formed in an age in which a dominant vision of human reality is shaped by Descartes's "I think, therefore I am." This vision of life inevitably diminishes, or even disregards, the reality of our bodies. My early Christian formation mostly focused on thinking and affirming right ideas about God and God's ways. This involved reading the Bible (something I still love to do daily) and making sure I understood what it was talking about.

Our worship services were mostly sitting in a room with rows of chairs listening to someone else speak. Our bodies were mostly simply what got us into the room. We didn't understand Christians in other traditions who stood up or sat down or kneeled in unison. It seemed silly to us—apparently rote activities with little relevance to our lived experience. We seemed to understand ourselves mostly as intellectual boxes into which right ideas and affirmations were being deposited.

How does this affect the issue of anxiety? In part, I got used to dealing with my life only by thinking about it, or trying to think differently or better about it. There was a practical detachment from the physical realities of living. It was as though there were a buildup of energy that leaked out, in part, as physical sensations of anxiety. But bodies matter. Incarnation is a basic divine reality. I can learn to live the peace of God in this gift of a body.

THE GOD WHO PROVIDES

Gem and I often set aside twenty-four hours to get away together to a nearby retreat center. This has been a strategic element of our personal and ministry rhythm for decades now. Once, as we were sitting outside our rooms talking and praying, letting our minds be attentive to whatever God's Spirit seemed to bring our way, we noticed a peacock had walked into the outdoor hallway across the way. It began to drink from water that was sitting in a crack in the sidewalk. We could see the little ripples in this unlikely stream each time he drank. A bit later, we watched as a squirrel scampered out onto the lawn and located a pinecone. We watched him nibble away for ten minutes or more, scale by scale, locating the nut inside and enjoying it.

I remembered again the words of Jesus about the futility of worry in light of the care of the Father for us: "See how the flowers of the field grow. They do not labor or spin. Yet I tell you that not even Solomon in all his splendor was dressed like one of these" (Matthew 6:28-29). Flowers and animals aren't harried to produce what makes them beautiful; they welcome what they need as unearned abundance. This still requires effort. The peacock needed to walk over, lean down, and drink. The squirrel needed to search the lawn, pick up the pinecone, and chew away. But their work is done with provision they didn't produce.

Do I see my work like this? Do I assume that what I need is simply there if I will go out and look for it? Do I trust that there are unexpected streams of water and unseen bundles of provision waiting to be discovered if I will but seek? I can live this way and work this way: un-anxious, confident in divine provision rather than fearful of likely scarcity. I can work hard without working worried.

PRAYING WITH THE BODY

I'm learning a way of following Paul's counsel: "In view of God's mercy, to offer your bodies as a living sacrifice, holy and pleasing to God—this is your true and proper worship" (Romans 12:1). Worship is not just a mental exercise of thinking proper thoughts. Paul invites us to the physical act of offering our very bodies, alive and available, to God. This is the body's singular (holy) purpose and this pleases our Father in heaven.

One way I've been seeking to be trained by this practical instruction is to follow the ways that the Psalms invite us to engage with God in our very bodies. Think of how many ways a psalmist expresses worship as an offering of their body in some particular way (emphasis added):

- "Clap your *hands*, all you nations." (Psalm 47:1)
- "*Shout* to God with cries of joy." (Psalm 47:1)
- "In your name I will lift up my *hands*." (Psalm 63:4)
- "With *singing lips my mouth* will praise you." (Psalm 63:5)
- "Come, let us *bow down* in worship." (Psalm 95:6)
- "Let us *kneel* before the Lord our Maker." (Psalm 95:6)
- "I *stand* in awe of your laws." (Psalm 119:120)
- "I lift up my *eyes* to the mountains." (Psalm 121:1)
- "Praise him with timbrel and *dancing*." (Psalm 150:4)

The Psalms assume our physical engagement in worship. How different from a habit I've had, to mostly *think* my prayers or read the Scriptures to myself. Sometimes, the lack of bodily engagement with God has seemed to be a way of letting physical energy back up. This can end up arising in me as anxious thoughts and sensations. Even praying out loud rather than inwardly engages my lips, my mouth, my lungs. There is a literal vibration of my voice in my chest. Speaking my prayer aloud offers the energy of my body to God.

I'm growing in my experience of literally offering my body as a living sacrifice. I agree with the counsel but am still growing in that skill. I am learning how this works itself out in my physical life. Too often, I catch myself sitting still, mostly reading the Scriptures in my own head and praying quietly. This isn't wrong, but it doesn't engage my God-given body in worship.

I've been experimenting in solitary prayer with offering my body to God by sometimes standing when I pray. When I pray with the Benedictine monks who live nearby, they stand whenever they pray the words of the Gloria. And they bow together when they are addressing the Trinity, "Glory be to the Father and to the Son and to the Holy Spirit, as it was in the beginning, is now, and ever shall be, world without end. Amen." As I pray the office from the Book of Common Prayer, I'm experimenting with standing and bowing as an expression of my own reverence and praise.

When I offer my prayer of confession, I sometimes kneel as we do in our weekly gathering for worship in church. I may stand up and raise my hands when I express some word of Psalm praise or pray the Apostles' Creed. I may lift up my eyes as I pray one of the Psalms for morning prayer. There isn't anything magical or mystical about this; it is simply that in addition to loving the Lord with my mind and heart, I am expressing that love through the offering of my body to God in these practical, simple ways.

GUIDED BY ENERGY OR LACK OF ENERGY

Psychiatrist and spiritual director Gerald May talks about how he learned to pay attention to how energy (or a lack of it) was often a helpful guide to holy activity. He said, "It is difficult to describe the deep sense of guidance I experienced at times like that. I give words to it: yes, no, this, not that, now, not yet. But it doesn't come in words, nor even in thoughts. It's more like a kind of energy in a certain direction when the time is right for something, and a fatigue in that direction when it's not. Nature guided me, I think, by energy and lack of energy."[3]

There was a time when this thinking would have sounded odd or even out-of-bounds to me. Too subjective. Not theologically sophisticated enough. But I've had the same experience as Gerald May. There have been times when I've tried to push through a lack of energy for something, only to discern that this something didn't need as much attention as I assumed.

Energy is God's idea. There is no energy apart from the creative work of God. Paul prays that his brothers and sisters in Ephesus would be strengthened with power through God's Spirit in their inner being (Ephesians 3:16). I've learned, at times, to discern the direction in which God's Spirit is strengthening and empowering me, and the direction in which God is not. This doesn't have to be a cover for laziness. It has more often been helpful guidance for engaging in the work that God has prepared for me to walk in (Ephesians 2:10). Noticing the presence of holy energy, its direction and flow, seems to me a perfectly good way to describe our experience of cooperating with the work of God.

A LOST AND HIDDEN PRIZE

I grew up not far from the American River in Sacramento. Skipping stones, rafting, and lizard hunting marked my childhood years. Once, Grandpa Andy and my cousin Norman came to visit in the summer. Grandpa loved to fish, so one day we all went down to the river to fish for steelhead trout. As a junior higher, I wasn't a huge fan of fishing, but I always loved being near our neighborhood river.

Arriving at a favorite local spot, we put in our lines. Norman and I set our poles on the bank in a couple of staked holders and went off for our more preferred activity: tadpole, frog, and crawdad hunting.

We'd left our lines for a while, so when we returned, we found our two poles had become only one. Norman asked Grandpa, "Did you take my pole?" Grandpa looked a bit concerned because he hadn't. Norman turned to me and asked the same thing, but I'd been his partner in critter hunting for the last few hours.

So we all decided that Norman's pole had probably been pulled in by a big fish and was a lost cause, sad but probably true. But Norman didn't give up. He went back to the truck and got a fly-fishing pole (we'd been bait fishing) and started casting it in hopes of somehow catching the line from the lost pole. It seemed like a child's fantasy that anything would come of his efforts.

But after about thirty minutes, he had hooked a line. He looked over at me, wondering if he'd tangled with my line, but it wasn't out at the moment. And Grandpa wasn't fishing near us. So he hand-pulled that line until, believe it or not, he found his lost pole on one end of it. He then reeled in the line until, on the hook end of it, he brought in one of the biggest steelhead trout I'd ever seen. The poor thing was exhausted from fighting for hours against hook, line, and pole.

That story has entered our family lore. It reminds me how good it is when we think we've lost something to resist the temptation to give up. We can seek and lean in a bit, and perhaps recover what we were sure we'd lost.

Finding peace in my present and for my future has sometimes felt like that lost pole. I learned the way of anxiety so early in my life that I've wondered if I would ever find my way to overcoming it. But as I've leaned into it, I've found that not only am I finding my way to overcoming anxiety more often than I'm overcome by it, but I'm discovering a deep and rich treasure of peace that is more precious to me than I can describe. It's like that prize steelhead that lay hidden in the depths that my persistent cousin recovered.

NON-ANXIOUS REFLECTION

- Take a few moments to simply enjoy the creation that surrounds where you live. What qualities of God's presence did you discern? If you haven't in a while, when might you give yourself the gift of enjoying what God has made?

- In what ways does the idea strike you as mundane, that to abide in Christ is like a branch remaining connected to a vine? In what ways might the everyday reality of abiding be a gift rather than a boring hindrance?

- In your own life of prayer or engagement in Scripture, to what degree is your body involved? Do you feel drawn to experiment with standing, kneeling, or expressing prayer in other ways with your body? Notice what happens when you do.

12

RHYTHMS OF PEACE

My anxiety has often been rooted in a kind of soul arrhythmia. A healthy heart beats at a reliable rate. It seeks a regular rhythm of contraction and rest. Its rate may increase when we work harder, and it may slow when we are at rest. But a steady heart rhythm is a sign of a healthy person. Heart arrhythmia is when it beats too quickly, too slowly, or irregularly.

Soul health, I've found, is when the pace of my soul fits the flow of my life. There are times to be quick (though not hurried). There are times to be slow (though not sluggish). But sometimes my soul is faint or my soul is anxious. It's a kind of arrhythmia that is counter to peace, but there are healthy rhythms that have helped me find greater peace in my soul, my friendships, my work. There is a way of regulating our souls through holy, life-giving rhythms of life and work through the following practices.

SOLITUDE AND SILENCE

A few summers ago, we took the month of July as a minisabbatical.[1] Being authors and self-employed, we've come to realize we need this sort of break to sustain the level of writing and other content creation we're committed to. Retreat space and time like this has become a holy and life-giving habit for us since our twenties. This sabbatical began with a week on beautiful Orcas

Island, the largest of the San Juan Islands in the far northwest of Washington State.

One day, we decided to walk down to the shoreline and each spend the morning alone with God. Sitting on a log right by the water, I felt the warmth of the morning sun on my right side as I looked out over the bay. I listened to the lap of little waves landing on the pebbly coast; there was something so calming about the rhythm.

Even though I have been practicing this sort of extended retreat for solitude and silence, I still feel the resistance rise in me. It's good for me to notice it, because it is by definition a resistance to good rather than a resistance to evil. I still wrestle with this practice that has been a place of deepening my communion with God. Sometimes, I think my resistance is a buildup of avoiding the realities of my life. I let hurry rush me past honesty with God.

There are beautiful divine realities that I need to embrace. There are destructive realities that I need to acknowledge, confess, and repent of. Repent. That's a good word for the movement to which the Spirit is often inviting me. Repent is not a word just for addressing major failings. It is a word of gentle turnings, again and again, to face God, to walk in the light of God, to come out of my habits of hiding and escaping.

Our lives can be so full of interaction. Our souls need moments of solitude. Our lives can be so noisy. Our souls need moments of silence.

STILLNESS

To solitude and silence, I've found that it helps to add stillness. My favorite encouragement in Scripture is this direction to "be still, and know that I am God" (Psalm 46:10).

I'm grateful for the gift of the Psalms, especially in my morning and night prayer practices. They so often refresh in me a deep sense of God-with-me. Psalm 46 has been among my favorites over the years. It begins with a simple line: "God is our refuge and strength, an ever-present help in trouble" (v. 1).

It helps when I focus on those first two simple words: "God is." When it comes to finding rest in my restlessness, peace in my worries, this is where I'm invited to begin. "God is" is more than a statement of God's existence. It is a statement of presence. What I've come to see is that my inner anxiety and my proclivity to worry has a different implicit foundation: "God isn't." This is simply a way of recognizing that when anxiety is flourishing in my heart and mind, these are times when my sense of "God is" has worn thin.

My anxiety hints that God isn't caring, God isn't protecting, God isn't providing, God isn't making much of a difference in my life. But in this Psalm, we can rehearse a better reality: God really is our refuge—a place of comfort, of abundance, of provision. God really is our strength when we feel beat up by everything that concerns us. God actually is always present to help us in any and every trouble we face. My anxiety has a way of highlighting troubles and dimming my awareness of "God is."

As the Psalm continues, we come to a beautiful image: "There is a river whose streams make glad the city of God, the holy place where the Most High dwells" (v. 4). When I'm tempted to see troubles in my life as though they were a tsunami and God were a ripple, the psalm writer paints us a picture of a rushing river that refreshes and rejoices us in God's presence. Again, anxiety magnifies troubles and seeks to overpower my simple awareness of God's powerful, good presence with and in me. God really is with us to help us. Rehearsing this reality helps me remember and grow confident.

The Psalm comes to a place of specific invitation: "Come and see" (v. 8). From places of feeling overwhelmed by fears or anxieties, I'm invited to come and look. At what? At what God has done. God isn't overwhelmed by my troubles. Actually, the reverse is true. God "makes wars cease to the ends of the earth. He breaks the bow and shatters the spear; he burns the shields with fire" (v. 9).

I can notice God-with-me amid that which troubles me. Troubles sometimes seek to overwhelm or intimidate me. I can imagine God dwarfing those troubles by his powerful, helpful presence. I can envision God's help in the places I feel helpless. Helplessness and hopelessness have always amplified my anxieties.

This psalm journey finally brings us to the well-known command that is among the most difficult to follow when we are deeply anxious: "Be still, and know that I am God" (v. 10). This isn't the psalm writer talking with us *about* God. This is God speaking to our very hearts and souls. This is God in his power and peace inviting us to be encouraged by his presence. When our anxiety would provoke us to frantic activity, God would invite us to stop and look to him. "Be still. Remember me."

Reflecting on the element of stillness and anxiety, I've learned that when anxiety wants to make me run somewhere, whether in fight or flight, it is often most helpful to be still. Sometimes the best response in a moment of strong anxious feelings is to just stop, to be still, to be silent, to let the anxious thoughts float through without arguing with them, solving them, or examining them. There is a way of engaging my anxious thoughts that leaves me on the turbulent surface of my life. But there is also a way of sinking down into that place of stillness in my soul where Christ has made himself at home.

"The LORD Almighty is with us; the God of Jacob is our fortress" (v. 11). We are not alone in our troubles. We are not isolated before that which threatens us. We are in the presence of a mighty Helper. Stillness is a way to notice presence.

SAMENESS

As I sat on that shoreline, I also felt a familiar boredom rising in me. I'm accustomed to a lot of stimulation in my life, and sitting still for that long felt boring. But I realized that boredom in such a moment might be a gift—a holy thing, maybe even an element of spiritual training—rather than an affliction.

I've long been familiar with practices of solitude (refraining from usual company), silence (refraining from usual interactions), and stillness (refraining from usual activities). Perhaps I should add *sameness* (refraining from usual levels of mental or physical stimulation) to that list.

Part of the discipline of solitude and silence for me is simply to rest in a place of non-productivity, to enjoy what *is* without improving or further developing it in one way or another. I still resist this because of my deep instinct that "I am what I do." I find myself resisting the sameness of such a practice. The discipline is to let this compulsive productivity orientation wear itself out. I can sit and look at what is in all that God has made. I do not need to make something of it, prove something, or create something more.

I've found, over time, that deep inner peace is a fruit grown from often following Jesus to a lonely place to offer God the gift of my attention, to seek communion, to pray. I find that I am able to bring that peace back with me into my busy life. I engage my full work schedule more and more from a soul at rest in God. There grows in me a peace that arises from my growing communion with God. I let retreat train me in peace when the world around me seems bent on training me in fear, worry, greed, or urgency.

That morning on Orcas Island, I experienced sameness as I heard the steady rhythm of little waves lapping the rocky shore. It was the same sound minute after minute, hour after hour. I experienced comforting sameness as I saw the unchanging scene before me—a mostly glassy bay, other islands fading into lighter shades of gray the more distant they were, the gray blue of the Sound—all unchanging.

I could change my narrative about boredom and decide to experience it as a gift. Sameness could be a way of leaning into the sort of receptivity for how God may wish to move, speak, or reveal himself to me. I could receive boredom as God-given instead of as negative. It might be a place of calm, of rest, of peace for my soul. Perhaps some boredom on a retreat day or in a sabbatical season is the sort of withdrawal that is necessary to my recovery.

We live in a time when most of us crave immense variety. We feel we must remain stimulated, and we resist anything that feels monotonous or uniform. When we have a moment without immediate responsibility, we often bring our phone to our face. This rhythm doesn't usually lead to peace. So the practice of sameness might be among the harder disciplines for us these days.

We are so used to high levels of mental and emotional stimulation. The average young adult today would be perturbed by the low levels of stimulation that were normal for me in my own young adulthood, an era before the omnipresent devices that now fill our lives. Sometimes our souls may need to practice sameness to become inwardly still enough to notice the movement of God.

One of the practices that has helped me sink into this sort of retreat is to creatively engage the Lord's Prayer from Matthew 6:9-10 "Our Father in heaven, . . . your kingdom come, your will be done, on earth as it is in heaven." I focus that prayer on various aspects of myself by adding a phrase.

Lord, your kingdom come and your will be done

In my mind as it's done in heaven (so that God rules over my thoughts);

In my heart (so that God may reign in my intentions);

In my arms (so that God might be my strength);

In my hands (so that God might guide my every action);

In my feet (so that I might go with God each step of my journey); and

In my belly (so that my appetites, my hungers, and my thirsts might be filled in God).

This practice has a way of helping me sink into the sameness of retreat.

STABILITY

In addition to sameness, I'm also drawn to *stability* (refraining from constant change). Monastic stability is usually understood in terms of a monk or sister remaining in the same monastery, but it has broader implications. It is the intentional bias toward *staying put*—or remaining in one place—rather than seeking change for the sake of change. It's a purposeful resistance to the impulse that tells us "the grass is greener over there."

In retreat, stability is the practice of picking a location and staying put. While on retreat, I've sometimes spent a great deal of my time wandering the retreat center and seeking the perfect place to meet with God, when instead I could simply find a good, nearby spot and stay put. God really is everywhere. God is not more present in the perfect little nook of a retreat center than in a less ideal location.

Stability teaches me to notice God where I am rather than imagining that God is easier to notice somewhere else. Stability reminds me that exactly where I am is just where God is present.

SIMPLICITY

To solitude, silence, stillness, sameness, and stability, I would finally add *simplicity*, which is refraining from my usual complexity of life. Simplicity might look like not bringing too much with me on retreat. I've often been tempted to bring a backpack full of books to read, but perhaps one book is plenty. Maybe even bringing nothing and letting the book of God's creation speak to me would be helpful.

Author Esther de Waal suggests that

living the solitary life brings a lesson about the importance of structure, the framework, and orderliness that are vital in order to prevent solitude from breaking down into lassitude, untidiness, lethargy, depression. Each person living on his or her own discovers the cost of not running away, of staying still without giving up, of being totally present to God, one's own self and the place itself—which is stability, a way of living with truth. It is only too easy to speak longingly of the solitary life, of the beauty of silence and solitude (and I notice with a mixture of alarm and amusement the growing popularity of writing about solitude today) without facing its harsh reality.[2]

In these retreat practices of solitude, silence, and the rest, there is need for structure, a framework and orderliness. Without these, it is too easy for solitude and silence to degenerate into counterfeits of themselves like inertia, disorder, acedia, weariness, and even depression. Engaging solitude and silence involves "staying in your cell" rather than leaving, whether literally by exiting your room or virtually through running away into social media or other distracting escapes. I am invited to remain still, to be attentive to God (whether or not I sense God's presence), and to be present to myself and the present place and moment.

So on that rocky shore, I embraced the *solitude* that became an opportunity to experience the company of God. I welcomed *silence* as a place to hear the voice of God. I settled into *stillness* where I might discern the movement of God. I rested into *sameness* as the place where I might enjoy the creativity of God. I rooted myself in *stability* so that I might recognize the presence of God. And I sat in *simplicity* so that I might enter into the unity of God. So when it comes to the regulating practice of personal retreat, I find these elements help me:

- Solitude: Find a place to be alone with God. Follow the pattern of Jesus who often withdrew to lonely places to pray. (Luke 5:16)

- Silence: Resist the temptation to overthink things. Cultivate a listening posture.

- Stillness: Let your body come to rest. Be attentive to the presence and movement of God.

- Sameness: Don't avoid what feels like negative boredom. Let sameness be a kind of blank canvas on which God can express creativity. Resist the temptation to distract yourself.

+ Stability: Find a good place and stay put. Don't look for a better place than the one you've chosen. Remember that God is always with you right where you are.

+ Simplicity: Don't bring a lot with you. Don't assume that a backpack full of books and other projects to fill your time is the main goal. Give yourself the gift of some tech-free time. Let divine fullness meet you in what may feel like emptiness.

Cultivating these countercultural rhythms has helped me practice deeper peace, inward and outward. Each is a movement against the tendencies of our contemporary culture and toward the values of God's peaceable kingdom.

SABBATH AND RETREAT

When I facilitate retreats for leaders, I often speak to them about the gift of *sabbath*; it is a sort of retreat built into God's design of creation.

I was once encouraging a group of pastors on retreat together in Rwanda of the divine invitation that sabbath is to us. I was sharing with these bivocational pastors that observing a weekly sabbath is actually more fruitful than remaining engaged in our work seven days a week.

The idea of not working one day a week could sound like a crazy and impractical idea from a privileged Westerner like myself—I get that. But we are paying the price for our overwork when we don't incorporate sabbath into our lives, whether we live in North America or in Rwanda, where there is an increase of prosperity in urban settings. In my work around the world, I observe that we are exporting our patterns of overwork—but not the practice of sabbath—to many around the globe.

It's important to determine whether sabbath is simply a sectarian rule for a particular group of religious folk in history (the Jews), an option for the privileged, or whether it might be a rhythm built into the very fabric of creation. As I read the language about sabbath in the Hebrew Scriptures, I see it as an invitation to a way of life that works and not as a religious distinctive with little practical effect. Sabbath, for example, was meant to be the great equalizer between rich and poor. It was slaves in Egypt who hadn't been able to observe the Sabbath who God then urged to keep the Sabbath holy; God would provide for them. Those with much could bless those with little, especially on the day when the whole community rested.

As I continued to interact with these very busy and faithful pastors in Rwanda, I tried to find a way that sabbath would sound like a gift and an invitation to their ears rather than as an impossible, useless idea. One of the things I've often said to leaders in the United States is that I can get more done in six days than I can in seven. Maybe it sounds a little trite, but it's really true. My own overwork has not been nearly as fruitful in a way that lasts as my work rooted in sabbath rest has been.

So I decided to experiment on a whiteboard with this group of Rwandan leaders. I drew a seven-column image that represented a week's schedule. I asked them what quality of work we accomplish when we work day after day, getting more and more tired. I asked them to suggest a percentage between 0 percent (getting nothing done) and 100 percent (working at our very best). They suggested they probably worked at about 40 percent capacity when they were exhausted.

I then did a little theoretical math problem with them. If they work seven days at about 40 percent capacity, how many full, fruitful days of work are they actually doing? Forty percent of seven days is a bit less than three days. (I'm sure a math professor will tell me that this isn't how the mathematics of work works, but it's more of a metaphor than a formula.)

I then drew the same weekly schedule but asked if they had a full sabbath day to rest, enjoy their family, and be refreshed and restored, what might be the quality of their work in those other six days? They spoke among themselves and suggested that it might be more like 80 percent of their capacity. I suggested that if indeed they worked at 80 percent on six days, that might be the equivalent of nearly five full, fruitful days of work.

I was simply trying to help them see that our work is at its most fruitful when it grows in a rested soul, when it is the fruit of refreshed and deepened communion with God. These pastors saw what I meant and determined to experiment with finding a day each week (or part of a day) when they might try on God's invitation of sabbath. I was so grateful and humbled.

I don't mean to turn sabbath into a utilitarian practice. I just mean that our life and our work is better when we cooperate with the nature of kingdom reality. Sabbath is an element of that reality. We were not made to define ourselves primarily in terms of our work. We were made for relationship, and work is one of the many good ways we enjoy relationship.

Simply put, who will do better work? The one who is tired, burdened, and overwhelmed, or the one who is at peace, refreshed, and energized? I know the answer in my own experience: the practice of sabbath over time has contributed powerfully to my learning how to actually do my work restfully, to bring a sabbath soul into the heart of my daily work.

On another leadership retreat, I was speaking to a group of Baptist pastors and their spouses in St. Petersburg, Russia. Like many Baptist Christians I've known (this was my faith tradition for decades), they didn't have a category for sabbath as an active practice in their life of faith. They tended to think of sabbath as an Old Testament thing that didn't have New Testament implications.

But before Sabbath (the Jewish holy day) was a Mosaic Law, it was a rhythm of creation. Before Sabbath was a pharisaic legalism, it was a divine gift. Jesus embodied the sabbath (the practice of rest) so that, in following him, we could enter into his rest. He didn't ignore the Sabbath; he fulfilled it in his way of life. An anxious shepherd will not likely do well leading their sheep to green pastures or quiet waters—and this is where people need to be led these days. People are desperate for the experience of peace. Because burnout, anxiety, and drivenness are so life destroying in our day, it just might be that rest for our souls is the very best facet of Jesus' good news of the kingdom.

But too many Christian leaders have a very restless way of life and work. They have come to believe in a Jesus who seems more Boss than Friend. Too many have come to see their work as demanded rather than given, a matter of human responsibility before it is a matter of divine generosity. This is like dragging a wheelbarrow upside-down. We are invited to work hard rather than work hurried, but there is no need to make our work *harder*. The yoke to which Jesus invites us is actually a good fit and not too heavy. When we rest in it with Jesus carrying the heavy end, we experience ministry as the sort of yoke Jesus described it to be.

God has given us the gift of a rhythm of living that will help us thrive. We can actually come to live into the abundant life Jesus lived and proclaimed. And rhythms of retreat and of sabbath will help us make our way forward in mighty ways.

NON-ANXIOUS REFLECTION

• Reflect on the six rhythms of retreat we've explored here (silence, solitude, stillness, sameness, stability, simplicity). Which feels most inviting? Which feels most challenging? Why?

• Which of these six rhythms might God be inviting you to explore in this season of your journey with Jesus? How might you do that in the near future?

• In the spirit of stability, might there be a way to engage in a sort of "retreat in place" at your own home, workplace, or church? If so, what might that look like?

• What do you think of the story about "sabbath math"? Does it ring true to your experience? If so, how does it move you in relation to your own current practice of sabbath, whatever that might be?

13

NON-ANXIOUS WORK

In his upper room conversation with his inner circle, Jesus shared wisdom and vision for his friends to help them navigate a future they couldn't imagine. In as many ways that Jesus hinted at his suffering and death, they couldn't fathom such a thing. He wanted them to realize that what seemed to be the end of their shared work will only be the beginning. At one point, he talked about the union he and the Father share, and how his followers might participate in this fruitful communion through trust and prayer.

> Believe me when I say that I am in the Father and the Father is in me; or at least believe on the evidence of the works themselves. Very truly I tell you, whoever believes in me will do the works I have been doing, and they will do even greater things than these, because I am going to the Father. And I will do whatever you ask in my name, so that the Father may be glorified in the Son. You may ask me for anything in my name, and I will do it. (John 14:11-14)

As he did with his inner circle that night, Jesus invites us to believe him—to trust him—when he says that he is in the Father and the Father is in him. The Father and the Son could not be closer to one another. If we struggle to trust the words of Jesus, we can at least trust what we see in his life and ways.

In this trusting, we discover that we can work with Jesus in the same Spirit as he worked (and works) with the Father. Together, we can accomplish in this world the very same sort of work that we read of in the Gospels.

GREATER THINGS

Jesus further said that we may do even greater things, through trusting collaboration, than he did. I don't think Jesus is daring us to outdo him in signs or miracles. I believe he envisions a world full of women and men who have learned to work fruitfully *with* him in humble confidence. What a beautiful multiplication of that which Jesus began two millennia ago.

These greater things aren't works we do *for* God at a distance from God. They are countless ways that all those who declare allegiance to Jesus might work with him in the power and under the guidance of the Spirit, to extend the goodness of his kingdom throughout the world. I don't think Jesus is primarily envisioning enormous organizations as the fulfillment of his vision. I believe he envisions countless individual followers living in loving, responsive fellowship with him and one another wherever they live and work. How much greater is the fruit of this sort of worldwide effort?

In all that we do, God is inviting us in Christ to trust in him and not in ourselves. When I focus on my own efforts or capacities, anxiety often increases within me. It is always tempting to focus more on our capability to follow than on God's power to lead. Trust is a relational invitation. We aren't being asked to believe things *about* God so much as to lean with trust on the presence of God-with-us. Here, we learn to work with the God of peace in peace. Rather than trying to wrap our arms around something too big for us, we work alongside the One whose capacity is measureless.

In terms of this "greater things" insight, Jesus could be in only one place at a time in the days of his earthly life. Now, as Jesus is seated at the right hand of the Father in heavenly realms, he can be present all over the world by the Spirit. Jesus can do far greater work in and through each of his disciples than he could in his single human body. Jesus wants to bless people through our lives as we learn to more deeply trust and closely follow him.

Remember that the primary work to which God has invited us is to help others learn to trust and follow Christ. All the tasks, structures, and organizational activities we find ourselves engaged in are meant to serve that end. As it relates to our way of working, Vincent de Paul, a seventeenth-century French priest dedicated to serving the poor, often talked about the temptation to "outstrip Providence" rather than following Providence.[1]

When I learn to walk with God and cooperate with grace, I find peace there to accompany me. When I try to run ahead of God's generosity, I find anxiety rises in me. Instead of imagining that Christ has given us work we're to run off to and accomplish on our own, it's better to imagine Christ inviting us into his friendship and, therefore, into collaboration with him. Grace empowers us for holy action, rooted in peace.

Perhaps the anxious resistance that rises in me is not an indicator of my inevitable failure in my work. It may instead be a sign of the importance of my work in the eyes of God. I do not have to let resistance be my boss. I can instead learn to make it work for me.

I believe Jesus wants us to deepen our communion with him and the Father. He wants us to find ourselves more at home in his reliable love, and then to live and work from this place. Working in the presence of grace and peace makes such a difference in the spirit of our heart and mind.

ANXIOUS WORK

I've come to realize that one of the reasons I let myself become engrossed in my work—not so much as an expression of my communion with God but as a self-focused activity—is to avoid or escape unpleasant dynamics in my own life. I have pursued work for God to escape the face of God.[2] A lot of my own work is creative and information oriented. Edwin Friedman suggests that "the chronic anxiety in American society has made the imbibing of data and technique addictive precisely because it enables leaders not to have to face their selves."[3]

In my work, I've found that an anxious orientation can get me so wrapped up in my own ideas, theories, visions, or plans that I fail to give sufficient attention to my *life*. But who I am as I do what I do makes an immense difference. And if Friedman's observation about anxiety was true at the end of the twentieth century, it's exponentially true of our reality a couple of decades into this new century.

The first year of the global Covid-19 pandemic was a study in how we deal (or fail to adequately deal) with our anxieties. Like fear, our anxieties provoke our aggressive impulses (fight), our tendency to escape and avoid (flight), or our urge to numb out and hide (freeze). In this, I've often found myself frantically working outside myself to solve a problem that is largely within myself. I project issues in me onto others, then react to them with all the energy that I could be directing toward my own restoration or recovery.

How much better it would be to lean into that which is unpleasant or misdirected in my life and live it in the presence of God's grace and mercy. I might discover that instead of avoiding or escaping my anxiety, I might learn how to make myself at home in divine peace.

THE UNEXPECTED IDOLATRY
OF WORKAHOLISM

I was recently stopped in my reading of Scripture by a line in Hosea:

> Assyria cannot save us;
>> we will not mount warhorses.
> *We will never again say "Our gods"*
>> *to what our own hands have made,*
>> for in you the fatherless find compassion.
>>> (Hosea 14:3, emphasis mine)

In this passage, Israel has awakened to their political idolatry. They had put their trust in Assyria for their protection instead of trusting in their God. Assyria exploited them instead. The line that arrested my attention was, "We will never again say 'Our gods' to what our own hands have made."

There is plenty of language like this about worshiping manmade idols of wood and stone. In the West, we see the silliness of this; at least we *think* we do. But we seem less sensitized to the implicit condemnation of workaholism in these words as well. We still have a way of worshiping the work of our hands, even if the outcome is not a material idol. We can find ourselves seeking our primary sense of identity and meaning in what we do to earn a living. We treat our work like it was our god.

Instead of looking for the source of our life in what we do, we can find joy in God. In this way we remember that our delight, our thriving, and our ultimate identity is rooted in God alone. I do not desperately need someone else to affirm the work I do to live in deep well-being. Outsourcing our identity in this way is a recipe for anxiety. We know somehow in the depth of our souls that finding a reliable identity in the work we do and how others respond to it is a fragile thing.

When we try to get from our work what only God can give, then we've made it an idol. In the end, God provides for us (truly, often it's through our jobs). But our jobs are a means God uses. Our work can no more save us or provide for the needs of our soul than an idol made of wood or precious metals can. It is a blind spot in our culture.

This sort of workaholism can especially arise in the lives of those who are involved in religious sorts of labor. I was in northeast India for a few days of leadership training for church leaders. In an afternoon session, I was emphasizing the idea that Jesus not only invites us to join him in his work, but he also invites us to join him in moments of rest.

We were making our way through this teaching when one of the pastors stood up and proclaimed with great enthusiasm that we are called to be faithful to the work of God until we die. (The spirit of the declaration sounded a bit more like "until it kills us.") It sounded very much like preachers I've heard in my own conservative Protestant past. His words of presumed encouragement were clearly counter to everything I'd been saying. He was talking about a faithfulness to ministry that preempts everything else. I could feel the heaviness that fell on the room.

I wrestled inside to find a way to affirm this elder statesman, but also surface what I felt was the flat side of his words. I sensed the Spirit nudging me to say, "When Jesus withdrew to lonely places to pray, was he obeying the will of the Father, or was he disobeying the will of the Father?" I looked at this older pastor's face as he processed my question, and I could see what looked to me like relief as he smiled and responded.

It felt like this brought a deep breath of hope and encouragement into the room. Jesus really does invite us to bear the load of the cross with him. Working with God can make great demands of us. But Jesus also invites us to rest in communion with him. God rests at the end of the creation story not because he's tuckered out from all that work, but because rest is a place of relationship and enjoyment. Our work is merely another way to enjoy conversational friendship with God.

OUR WORK EXPRESSES OUR LIFE

Therefore work that is more free of anxiety is work done in greater cooperation with God. It is the outward expression of an inward relational reality. It is work done in collaboration with the God who is with us rather than work done in isolation with hopes of God's blessing-from-a-distance somehow.

I was sitting in the dining room of an East Coast retreat center that overlooked an ocean cove; it was overcast at the moment, though it had been sunny the last couple of days. I had found a copy of Thomas Green's *The Friend of the Bridegroom* in the retreat house library, and I was encouraged as I read of an Ignatian vision of the contemplative life—it is that moment when God goes from being "he" to being "you."[4]

Contemplation is that moment when I can say from my soul, "The Lord is *my* shepherd." In our work, we work more free of anxiety as we grow more contemplative in our work. We work in an interactive conversation with God-with-us rather than for God as "him."

As I continued engaging with God on that retreat day, I returned to readings in Isaiah that had framed my week there. I read the words of love and hope God speaks to Israel in their exile, as words personally spoken to me in my own places of felt exile. As I engaged with the prophet, I realized that I sometimes have the habit of turning God's "I/you" statements into "him/them" statements. This creates distance where distance wasn't present. Sometimes it's my habit as a teacher to talk *about* God, when God is inviting me to be his child hearing the voice (and entering the presence) of my Father in heaven. Remembering myself in God's presence often refreshes my sense of just how peaceful God's presence is.

This collaborative way of engaging our work reminds me of Jesus' image for our interactive relationship with him: a yoke. A yoke is a way that two animals can work together to pull a plow or a wagon. *Yoke* language was also used to describe a disciple following a rabbi.

Jesus invited people to come to him if they found themselves weary and burdened, because he knew how to show them the way to rest; and then the shape the invitation took was a yoke. I'm thinking that some would have been a bit puzzled that Jesus' strategy for rest was an implement of work. But I can think of at least two ways that the yoke of Jesus is the perfect strategy by which we find rest for our souls.

First, we need to see ourselves in the yoke *with* Jesus. The yoke isn't something Jesus drops on our shoulders just before walking away to all the other important things he is taking care of. It is *his* yoke. He is bearing it, and he is inviting us to join him there. We come close to learn and to share in what he is doing. We are not working alone, but with him.

When I feel like I'm alone in the concerns I carry, my anxiety grows. When I feel isolated in the burdens I bear, my anxiety swells. When I remember I'm never alone in my responsibilities, or my cares, peace has a way of soaking more deeply into my soul and quieting my anxiety.

Second, it would have been common in the day of Jesus for a young, inexperienced animal to learn from a seasoned, well-experienced animal how to pull on the yoke. The seasoned animal would have been the one pulling the heavy end. I am not pulling the heavy end of the yoke that I am in with Jesus; he is. This is part of why his yoke is easy and his burden is light.

I might have imagined that Jesus' strategy for rest would have been a bed, or a comfortable chair, or a nice beach next to the Sea of Galilee. But instead he invites us to join him in his yoke. It's a way to stay close to him. It's a way to learn from him. It's a way to live my life and do my work, moment to moment with him, in more peace.

PERFORMANCE ANXIETY

A significant element of my own work is speaking to groups of leaders. In that, I have often wrestled with performance anxiety. I anticipate an upcoming engagement, experience feelings of anxiety, and assume that they are reliable predictors of how my time with those leaders will go. Anxiety, in this case, has nearly always been wrong. (I'd say *always*, but it's possible anxiety got lucky occasionally.) I've learned that such anxious feelings are not a helpful indicator of what is happening or going to happen.

When I speak or teach, the main thing happening is actually not my "performance." The main thing is that God's Spirit is at work—in and through me and in those who are listening. Anxiety focuses my attention on me. "Will I make myself clear?" "Will I say things they appreciate?" Or worse, "Will I impress those who are listening?" This is the way of anxiety.

But if I turn my attention away from worries about how I'll do when I speak, and toward the God who will be with me as I serve the people I've come to serve, I find that my anxieties begin to unwind and quiet. I am not there to be served (in terms of my ego or my sense of value); I am there to serve and to give what God wishes to give through my words.

I still experience nervous feelings rising when a speaking engagement is on the horizon. I'm learning that as noisy and insistent as those feelings are, they have been wrong too often to trust them. I can notice those feelings with compassion, but resist the temptation to follow their counsel.

In our work, we can learn to be less self-conscious and more God-aware. The former grows the weeds of worry. The latter is a garden of peace. I learn to think about how I might do good for others rather than how my work benefits or reflects on me. I've found that seeking and even praying for the good of others in the work I do has a way of being a kind of anxiety repellent. Praying for the good and the flourishing of another hits at the root of anxiety.

SPIRITUAL FORMATION ISN'T HURRIED

When it comes to non-anxious work, I love the simple tagline that we've developed to share the message, values, and way of our nonprofit for spiritual formation and leadership coaching. We teach leaders how *resting deeper* and *living fuller* in the spirit of Jesus and his kingdom will result in *leading better*. Often though, when we travel to speak to a group of leaders those who have control of the training schedule want to pack as much lecture as possible into our time together. They want me to back up my content dump truck and unload as much information as I can humanly manage in our limited time. I get it—we've often traveled hours, if not days, to be together. I once led a training for Indian leaders who had been on trains for three days to attend a training in Pathankot in the far north of the country.

But what we must remember is that the *way* that we teach and train is as important as *what* we teach and train. Teaching the ways of unhurried living in a packed schedule simply reinforces the hurried habits we are trying to expose. Those I train need a spacious setting to take in insights, reflect on them as they relate to their own experience, and perhaps even have time to imagine and envision how those insights might reshape their lives and work back home. (If we assume they'll have time to do this when they return to their already very busy lives, we've likely made a fatal assumption.)

Jesus had a bias for taking an unhurried apprentice approach to training rather than a quick and efficient lecture approach. Apprentices learn by watching, doing, and being mentored, not by listening, leaving, and trying to do it themselves. Jesus taught the crowds, but primarily to invite them into a closer relationship with him as Master. Jesus apprenticed the Twelve and the seventy-two closely. People not only need to learn *what* Jesus taught, but they need to see how Jesus lived and led, modeled by leaders who have embodied the ways of Jesus over time.

So when I come to train leaders in an unhurried way of living and leading, it doesn't work to provide that training in a schedule that is packed with meetings and filled with lectures. We need space to reflect on what we are learning. We need space to try it on. We need space to interact with and learn from others. We need time to decide our intentions for how we will live out what we are learning when we return to our life and leadership back home. This is an unhurried *way* to teach unhurried living.

I'm encouraged that much of the feedback we've received from groups of leaders we've trained is usually not about what we are teaching, but about how we teach. We create a restful schedule. We build in space for personal and group reflection. We make sure people have a chance to talk with one another about what they are learning, thinking, and feeling.

The "secret sauce" is giving people time to try on what they are hearing. Too many of us attend conferences, get pumped up, and then go home to our busy lives and forget or don't make time to implement what we learned. There must be time when we're gathering to experience what we teach. We share an insight. We give a bit of guidance for individual reflection and experimentation. We regather to debrief what was helpful and what wasn't. We make space for questions and responses. This is what fruitful training looks like. Storing up immense amounts of unprocessed and unpracticed insight is only going to provoke anxiety. Guiding people to practice the wisdom of God leads to peace.

Personal transformation that leads to peace doesn't happen in the collecting of more information. Knowledge without practice doesn't lead to wisdom or peace. Wisdom is knowing how truth works by experience.

Once when I was in an African country to provide unhurried leadership training for a group of pastors, there was a world-renowned Christian leader in the country at the same time. I had a couple dozen leaders; his gatherings had two thousand leaders. I learned that the topic of one of his talks was the importance of rest. Since many African leaders I've met have taken on the driven, over-busy ways of their North American brothers and sisters, it's an important message.

But this leader gave his message of rest to pastors in a crowded conference setting with a compressed schedule. They had no opportunity to have even a taste of what he was sharing. Rest was also inhibited by the event being led by busy, efficient leaders who didn't seem to be practicing what was being preached. How many of those African leaders do you think made their way to the actual practice of a more restful ministry schedule, especially given the very busy lives to which they would return after the conference closes? The message was helpful, but the way it was given wasn't.

In our little gathering of a couple dozen leaders, we were also sharing a theology of rest. You could call it a "rest ethic" to balance our strong work ethic. But we also arranged the schedule to make space for unhurried time in God's presence and in interactive community. After a few hours like this, we witnessed that participants were growing in the wisdom of what they were learning. They had a taste of something good to which they had high intentions and vision for returning to back at home.

If we have an opportunity to sit and listen to a well-known and respected leader, our instinct is to want them to talk every minute we're together. We hope that hearing them speak will change us, perhaps almost automatically. But wisdom is more likely to find a resting place in us if they share their wise way of living and leading, then we try it on ourselves while we're together, interacting with others about how we are learning, struggling, and so on. A seed would have actually been planted and watered in our souls.

The rhythm of how we learn and live is critical. I believe deeply in the insights and ideas about unhurried living that I share; I also believe that the way these truths are planted in the hearts of the leaders we train involves more than giving well-crafted presentations. We train people not just in what Jesus said, but in how Jesus lived. We guide them in practicing the peaceful way of Jesus with guided experiences that we try on, reflect on, interact about, and receive mentoring in. This is training in the spirit of Jesus.

PRAYING MY WORK, WORKING MY PRAYER

A very simple way that I am learning to do my work in peace rather than out of anxiety is by praying my work and then working out my prayer. On evenings before a workday, I take time to pray through my intended work for the next day. I create a tentative plan for the day—a flow for the work as I envision it. I think about the people I expect to meet with. I welcome God's grace to be present to them now and when we meet. I think prayerfully about the projects and tasks I intend to engage. I welcome everything of God's generous grace he may wish to give me in that work. I pray my work in advance of it.

In this evening practice, there are regular or obvious tasks, projects, and meetings that will be part of my following day of work. But I often take to heart a line I read in *Evelyn Underhill's Prayer Book*: "Let us ask God to show us these things which He desires that we should do."[5] I will take some moments to be still and quiet, attentive to thoughts the Spirit may raise about work for the following day I hadn't considered. Sometimes people come to mind that I'll reach out to, or tasks or projects that weren't on my radar that I explore the next day. The work of God is bigger than my current vision of my work. God can make my sense of my work more spacious.

Underhill's prayerful phrase begins with the words "Let us." I've sometimes written my task list for a day as a list of phrases beginning with "Let's." I imagine it as a simple way of embracing God's invitation to work with him and my hope that we might collaborate through the course of the day.

This feels like a life-giving way to frame the hours of my workday. Instead of a burdensome list of overwhelming work, it feels like a vision of how I might spend my day working fruitfully together with God. I find myself hopeful rather than feeling swamped.

Then, in my morning prayer the next day, as I enter into my day of work, I review my plan prayerfully. Again, I look through the people, plans, and projects I expect to engage throughout the course of the day. I give thanks for the opportunities. I remind myself that I *get* to work rather than *have* to work. I envision what it will look like to enjoy the presence of God at work in and through me in each of those moments.

Sometimes, I'll take a moment to offer a brief and specific prayer in my journal for each task, project, or appointment I anticipate in the day ahead. What might I need from God to do this work well? What might I hope God will do in and through me at that particular point in my day? I may feel anxiety in advance of a hard meeting. I'll pray for God's peace to guard my heart and for a greater awareness that I'm not alone in that meeting. I often find myself far more energized and ready to engage my day when I pray my work in this way.

Work can be a source of great anxiety. What a blessing to learn to see work as a gift and as an opportunity to live in collaborative communion with God.

NON-ANXIOUS REFLECTION

- What relationship has anxiety had to your work? Are there ways it has driven you? Hindered you? Paralyzed you? Why not talk with God about this dynamic in your experience?

- Workaholism is one of the acceptable, if not rewarded, addictions in many organizational environments. Take a moment to think about some of the costs of such overwork. What insights do you gain?

- Experiment with the "praying my work, working my prayer" practice. When you've tried it on, what challenges did you experience? What fruit did you notice?

14

BECOMING A MASTER
OF PEACE

One of the moments I love most in an Anglican worship service is the closing sentence: "Go in peace to love and serve the Lord." I have this sense of being sent out into my life for the week ahead with peace attending my steps. It makes me think about the concern of Jesus that we would go in peace.

On the evening when Jesus had been raised and had changed everything, his disciples were hiding behind locked doors for fear of the Jewish leaders (John 20:19). They had barely escaped being arrested with Jesus in the Garden of Gethsemane. Maybe they were having a conversation about how best to escape the city without being seen by Roman authorities or the Jewish leaders.

Then Jesus came, on that evening of his resurrection. A week later, he came to be among them again when Thomas was present. I try to imagine how disorienting the events of Jesus' resurrection would have been to the frightened circle of disciples. We've had two thousand years to grow accustomed to and live into the reality of what happened. They had only known this news for hours. It would take them a while to more fully realize the hinge of history that day would become.

So on that resurrection eve, the disciples were hiding in fear. The Jewish leaders had made their intention quite clear when they provoked the crowd to join them in their call for the crucifixion of Jesus of Nazareth. They weren't going to treat the followers of Jesus any better. So Jesus came and stood among them. His first gift to them was simply his presence—his risen presence. He stood with them in the place of their fears.

RECEIVING THE PEACE OF CHRIST

The door that was locked in fear did not prevent the loving, joyful, peace-bringing presence of Jesus to be among them. And our own fears do not hinder Jesus. In the midst of our own fears, Jesus comes to be with us as well.

Jesus does not break down the locked door. He doesn't need to. The text simply says that he came, stood among them, and spoke four simple, mighty words: "Peace be with you!" These are more than just a wish or a hope. They are words of substance. Jesus is *giving* them his peace. He is speaking peace to their fears. He is speaking peace to their worries. He is speaking peace to their troubled hearts and minds. And Jesus speaks peace to our fears and worries, to our troubled hearts and minds. He didn't speak peace over those followers only once. The Gospel story says that "again Jesus said, 'Peace be with you!'" (John 20:21).

Worry and fear are not resolved in a single moment in our lives. At least they haven't been in my life. In seasons of challenge and radical change in our lives (and there have been a lot of them for me), we need Jesus to speak his peace to us many more times than once. He is a Prince of Peace. It is no trouble for him to speak peace into our lives as many times as we need him to.

Now, the disciples had heard their Master speak peace to them before. This was not a new idea for them. But they were in a new situation and needed to remember. Perhaps they would recall Jesus' words of peace to them in the upper room from a few nights earlier. He had said to them, "Peace I leave with you; my peace I give you. I do not give to you as the world gives. Do not let your hearts be troubled and do not be afraid" (John 14:27).

There is a difference between the peace the world offers and the peace that Christ gives. Peace in this world is sometimes about big promises that aren't usually kept well. "Buy this product and you'll enjoy peace and be anxiety-free." "Fill your life with consumables and you will be happy." The world gives peace that is situation dependent; or the peace this world offers is only available after our troubles come to an end, our problems are apparently solved, or our situation noticeably improves. The world gives peace that is resolution dependent.

But the peace of Jesus is *his* peace. Peace is his way of living. Jesus *is* the non-anxious presence. Jesus is not terrified by the things that terrify us. He knows the reality of the kingdom in ways we do not yet know them. He gives us peace by giving us himself. The peace of God is a Person. It is this Person who came to be among his disciples and to speak to them on the evening of his resurrection. What does his "Peace be with you" look like in lived terms? Listen to the words of Jesus to them: "As the Father has sent me, I am sending you" (John 20:21).

Peace is not just for their own sake. This peace he gave to them was also for the sake of others. In the same way the Father sent his Son into the world, Jesus was sending them ... and is sending us. He sends us into this world as a peaceful presence, as a non-anxious presence.

Doesn't it seem true that the world would be especially blessed if we were to go out into it as a peaceful presence—a non-anxious presence? Might that be one of the best gifts we could give in blessing to the world at a time when so many are terrified, when so many are letting their fears drive them to irrational behaviors? We can live our lives with peace because of the presence of the Prince of Peace among us, with us, in us.

And this sending is not the sort where we leave the presence of the Sender. Jesus breathed on that circle of disciples and said, "Receive the Holy Spirit" (John 20:22). God's very presence was with them every step of their journey from resurrection day forward. The Spirit of God is with us today and each day of whatever challenges us, worries us, even terrifies us.

WHEN DOUBTS COME

The Gospel continues to the well-known passage where we see "doubting Thomas" in action. The story goes that, for whatever reason, Thomas wasn't in the room on that resurrection evening when Jesus stood among the disciples and spoke those words of peace. Thomas hadn't witnessed that moment but had heard about it shortly afterward. He heard them say, "We have seen the Lord!" (John 20:25).

The Greek wording here carries with it a sense that the other disciples *kept* saying to him, "We have seen the Lord. We really have. It's not just a wishful tale. We are speaking as witnesses of reality." But it's more than Thomas could embrace. His anxiety, as it perhaps often did, was getting the better of him.

Thomas wanted to witness these things himself. He said, "Unless I see the nail marks in his hands and put my finger where the nails were, and put my hand into his side, I will not believe"

(John 20:25). Remember that Jesus had shown his hands and his side to the disciples that resurrection Sunday evening. He had wanted them to know that it really was him. Thomas hadn't been there to witness that, and he wanted to.

So it was a week later. What happened? The text literally says "eight days later" they are again gathered behind a locked door. The Jewish way of speaking about a span of days would have included the first and the last day of that span, so we're talking about the Sunday after the resurrection. The difference in this gathering is that Thomas was present this time. John, telling the story in his Gospel, uses the exact same phrasing: "He came and stood among them and said" (John 20:26). Jesus, in his grace, gave Thomas the gift of an opportunity to see and hear for himself what his fellow disciples had seen and heard a week earlier.

And Jesus was even more kind; he quoted Thomas's own words as an invitation. Touch the wounds on my hands, Thomas. Place your hand in the wound in my side, Thomas. I want you to trust me. I want you to rely on the reality of who I am and what has happened (John 20:27).

The passage doesn't say that Thomas stood there, arms crossed and suspicious as ever. It doesn't say that he reluctantly reached out to prove to himself that Jesus was really risen and present. The simple phrase that captures Thomas's response is worship, pure and simple: "My Lord and my God!" (John 20:28).

It's important to realize that "Lord" and "God" here were words a Jewish person would use only to describe the God of Israel. *Kyrios* and *Theos* are words reserved for divinity. Thomas moved from his deep doubts to declaring perhaps the profoundest faith in the room. Perhaps deep trust rose from the doubts that were the sign of his struggle to believe after his Master had been executed.

"My Lord and my God" is our most holy and fitting response to our own experience of Christ coming to be with us, speaking words of peace to us, sending us into the world just as the Father had sent him: that is worship. Humble, awe-filled, joyful worship. Worship is allowing the whole of our being to respond to the reality Jesus reveals to us of himself as the Risen One. Jesus comes to be among us, in our fears, with resurrection life. This is our proper worship of the Prince of Peace.

In response to Thomas's statement of worship, Jesus spoke a word of encouragement and hope that meets us where we find ourselves today. They are words that uniquely address us. He said, "Because you have seen me, you have believed; blessed are those who have not seen and yet have believed" (John 20:29).

We are not sitting in that room, two thousand years ago, witnessing the risen presence and hearing the risen word of our Lord. We are here. We have believed because we've trusted the testimony of those first followers who *did* witness the reality of the risen Christ. And they bore witness to other followers who trusted without being witnesses. And that testimony has been borne generation after generation until today.

So we are among those who are blessed to embrace the reality of resurrection in our lives on the strength of reliable testimony. We have tested the power of that reality in our own lives. We have experienced being risen to new life in communion with the Risen One. We have access, in this very moment, to the Prince of Peace among us.

The disciples were trying to find peace by hiding from the Jewish authorities behind a locked door. It doesn't look like their strategy worked very well. Perhaps it isn't too great a stretch to connect the locked door behind which the disciples hid with some of the ways we try to hide from troubles. Anxiety and fear tempt us in this way. In our places of trouble, real and antici-pated, Jesus speaks words of peace to us. "Peace be with you" is the way of Jesus with us. He doesn't treat us harshly with "Stop that worrying already!" He speaks peace to our troubled hearts and minds.

Think of your troubles in your present season. How would it feel if you experienced Jesus coming to you right here, speaking the words "Peace be with you" in this hard situation? My peace be with you. I will be with you as the Prince of Peace.

PEACE BE WITH YOU

What would it be like to live your life and engage your work with a more continual sense of the Lord of peace present with you all the time and in every situation? This is the very blessing Paul prayed at the close of his letter to his friends in Thessalonica: "Now may the Lord of peace himself give you peace at all times and in every way. The Lord be with all of you" (2 Thessalonians 3:16).

I love the blessing language of Paul in the New Testament. He says "may" the Lord of peace give you peace. There is a confi-dence in God's care and grace in that word. May peace be yours. Paul wants his friends in Thessalonica to experience the gift of peace given by the Lord of peace. He prayed with confidence that they might have deep peace in their hearts, their minds, and their relationships as a fruit of the presence of the Lord of peace with them.

There is no season or situation in which God's peace cannot reign over that which worries us, troubles us, challenges us. At all times and in every way, we can experience the peace of God reigning amid the anxious thoughts and feelings that tempt us.

And Paul learned that he could bless his friends with this peace. He experienced this peace reigning in his life, and he spoke words to extend that peace to them. He learned to live in peace, and he blessed them with this gift as well.

The words of Paul here are not merely a hopeful wish. "May" might sound to our ear like something that would be nice but is uncertain. But Paul's "may" expresses confident blessing rather than nice but feeble words of assurance. We also can speak words blessing others with peace, in the humble expectation that we are extending something substantially gracious to another, here namely peace.

When I was ordained as an Anglican priest a few years back, a friend who had been a priest for decades shared that one of the ministries to which I had now been ordained was the ministry of blessing. I was authorized by the church to speak words of blessing over people and even over things. I've taken that to heart in recent years. But the Lord Jesus has authorized each of us as members of his kingdom to speak words of blessing that are rooted in the real goodness of God's kingdom. We are able to actually give real peace to others through our words.

Again, Paul's words at the close of his letters can sound like an empty convention, like how we might end an email today with a quick "Sincerely, Alan." But I've come to see that Paul believed he was offering the blessing of real peace to his friends. To his friends in Rome he closed a letter, "The God of peace be with you all. Amen" (Romans 15:33). There is power in words of peace spoken with confidence in God's desire and ability to fulfill them. Paul believed he was, through the presence of Jesus among them by the Spirit, speaking words that would strengthen peace in their hearts, minds, and relationships.

God is inviting us to live more and more in the communion of his peace-filled presence. He is inviting us to then extend that peace to others in our relationships and to the world around us through our work. I believe this is God's primary strategy for bringing about peace in our world. He wants peace to be embodied in his people so that they might *live* peace in their worlds.

This becomes practical as I find ways to lean into my habit of anxiety. I'm learning to trust that what God says about worry's worthlessness is simply true. My worrying orientation has been a movement away from my trustworthy Friend. This is not a word of shame or condemnation. It's simply what I've come to discern about my habit of worry.

The writer of Hebrews suggests that outside a trusting orientation to God I can't live in the pleasure of God (Hebrews 11:6). In anxiety, I can't either. My habit of worry has had a way of blinding me to the measureless faithfulness of God-with-me. Not only is God real existentially, God exists here and now with me. My worries don't factor the reality of God-with-me into their assessment of my situation or my future.

One of my favorite passages of Scripture is found in the book of the prophet Zephaniah (3:17). I once took a little time to paraphrase it into a personal statement of faith:

> My God is always near
> His power is present to help me and save me
> God enjoys my presence
> His love calms my fears
> He sings with joy over me.

I find that my anxiety is not nearly as overwhelming when I hold this vision of God before my heart and mind. The God who is near me is for me. God enjoys me being near. God speaks words of love that quiet my turbulent thoughts. This is the God who is caring for me. And this God is a God of peace.

My anxiety arises within me like a confident preacher, declaring what it believes to be true about my present or my future. It claims to offer reliable counsel to me. But what if my anxiety is wrong and Jesus is right about my life? I'm learning not to assume that my feelings and thoughts of anxiety are good guides for my decisions or responses in life.

How would it affect my perspectives, my vision of work, my way of living if I were more aware of Jesus as Prince of Peace with me? Practicing the presence of the God of peace with me bears much better fruit than practicing the presence of anxiety. Learning to live in union and communion with the Prince of Peace has been producing more and more peace within me, in my interactions with others, and in the quality of my work.

Jesus is not the Prince of anxiety. Jesus is the Prince of Peace. The nature of Jesus is peaceful. The presence of Jesus is peaceful. He exercises authority as Lord of peace. Jesus as Prince of Peace does the work of peace in our living and in our working. I've found that my anxiety cannot produce the fruit of well-being. We must, as Jesus put it, "make the tree good." We need to work toward having healthy, whole, and peaceful lives that then bear the fruit of peaceful souls, peaceful relationships, peaceful work.

This is not to say that we will always walk around in a blissful cloud of felt well-being. We will find ourselves deeply concerned for the good of others. We will face situations that trouble us and provoke us. We will experience the concerns that are common to us all. We can, though, learn to face such situations in the assumption that the Prince of Peace has already been here, is at his peaceful work, and is inviting us into that work. Situations aren't omnipotent. God is. The God of peace is.

Jesus has invited us into his non-anxious friendship. We don't follow him at a distance. We don't live our life in a faraway land that he rarely visits. We follow Jesus as collaborators. The biblical term for this is "fellow worker." We can learn to stay alert and attentive to how Jesus responds to various circumstances as the Prince of Peace. This impacts the level of peace in our own thoughts and emotions. Jesus really is the ultimate non-anxious presence. Living in communion with him over time enables us to live more and more free of worry. This makes a non-anxious life possible.

CALLING ON JESUS

Remember where we first learn of Jesus as the Prince of Peace who would come? The prophet Isaiah speaks of a child who would be born, given to us as one to lead us. What is his name?

> And he will be called
> Wonderful Counselor, Mighty God,
> Everlasting Father, Prince of Peace. (Isaiah 9:6)

These four names for the One who would come are beautiful.

Isaiah says that he will be called *Wonderful Counselor*. The counsel he gives is better than the wisest and most experienced human counselor. It's certainly better than the counsel that my own anxiety offers. He speaks with wisdom that is deeper than we can plumb. He comes alongside us to enable us to make our way well in life, relationships, and work. Jesus' counsel is supernaturally insightful and wise. We find our way to peace by his astonishing guidance.

He will also be called *Mighty God.* Earlier in Isaiah's prophecy, Jesus is called *Immanuel* (7:14), or "God-with-us." Jesus is divinely powerful—infinitely capable. My anxieties don't overwhelm him. He is at work for our salvation, our deliverance, our liberation in all the ways we need. His might is not oppressive but protective. We find peace in his powerful care.

He will be called *Everlasting Father.* Though Jesus is Son to his Father in heaven, he is as a father to us. He is the best sort of father we might imagine. He fathers us with consistency and unfailing love. His care is powerful. We hear this title of Jesus echoing in his departing words in the last line of Matthew's Gospel to his disciples when he says, "And surely I am with you always, to the very end of the age" (Matthew 28:20). He is the sort of father who will never abandon us as some human fathers have done. We find peace in his reliable care.

Finally, he will be called *Prince of Peace.* His leadership is rooted in peace. He will go to war with that which seeks our harm, but war is not his primary aim. He is a Prince who seeks that which fulfills our true purpose and leads to our deep well-being. He is a Prince who creates a home for us that is non-anxious and fosters relational and communal harmony. His grace leads to our peace. He seeks our wholeness and our completeness. We find peace in him because he *is* peace.

I think again of the words of Jesus in the upper room: "Peace I leave with you; my peace I give you. I do not give to you as the world gives. Do not let your hearts be troubled and do not be afraid" (John 14:27). The peace Jesus offers us is not merely an idea. It is not simply a nice feeling we might have. Jesus gives us the peace of his presence. In the same way that peace is a fruit of God's Spirit (Galatians 5:22), peace is a quality of Jesus' person.

Remembering and trusting that Jesus is the Prince of Peace begins to transform my inner life. I learn to trust in this peace, more than I trust the anxieties that arise out of habit and unpleasant surprises. The peace of Jesus doesn't depend on a stress-free setting. It doesn't depend on things going the way I prefer. It doesn't depend on having only pleasant feelings moment to moment. The peace of Jesus is deep-rooted.

The peace that this world has on offer is fickle. If I have no problems, I might have peace. If I have lots of things, I might have peace. If trouble stays far from me, I might have peace. But even here I can imagine troubles or imagine that I don't have enough of something and lose that peace just as easily. Peace is not a reliable mark of the world around me. But Jesus is a Prince of Peace and he is with me.

If Jesus were to speak to me today as he did to those first disciples on that last night before the cross, I wonder if it might sound like this: "I am with you today, Alan, as the Prince of Peace. You are not alone. You are not abandoned. I am with you in whatever you do. Don't let your heart be troubled about the challenges that lie ahead of you. I am always with you. Remember this. Rehearse this reality more than you rehearse your anxious thoughts and feelings. Anxiety seeks to protect its place in your life. Don't let anxiety prevent you from learning to live a non-anxious life."

A PRAYER FOR ANXIOUS PEOPLE

I'm so glad you've taken this reading journey with me. I'm so grateful you decided to invest in the health of your own soul. There is hardly anything more important than that. I wonder what has been tempting you to anxious living these days. What losses have arisen? What challenges have crossed your path?

Jesus is inviting you to receive what you need from him. Sometimes, our first response to anxiety is to frantically do something. It's understandable. But Jesus often invites us first to receive something. His peace is a gift we can welcome and embrace. In this way, our practice of trust in him might grow. We might have a sense of God-with-us in the midst of that which has made our lives hard.

So in that spirit, I'd like to close this book with a prayer for you. First, I am thankful for you. I'm glad that God is the one who so wanted you that he chose you to come to him. I'm grateful that there are good things God has prepared in advance for you to enjoy and to share with others. I pray that your unhurried influence will grow, that you'll learn to work hard without working hurried.

I pray that you'll learn to work close with God rather than working far from God. May you learn to be active, but not hyperactive. May you learn to work at the pace of relationship, at the pace of love. May you have eyes to see the people under whom, alongside whom, and for whom you serve.

May you learn to be productive, but at the pace of peace. May you resist the temptation to be driven by anxious activity, but instead learn to join Jesus in the very fruitful work he is already doing around you. May you work hard, but at the pace of grace rather than at the pace of driven achievement. May you resist the temptation to outrun grace. May you learn to follow grace, to be strengthened by grace, to walk in grace.

When you are tempted to believe that this sort of influence is just not possible in your situation, may you gain a clearer vision of Jesus' holy and unhurried way of living and leading. May you grow in discernment so that you don't hurry ahead of where Jesus is already at work in and through you. May you live and work at the pace of rootedness. May this depth result in far greater fruit than frantic busyness will ever produce.

May you come to fix your eyes on Jesus, *the* non-anxious One. May you have the patience to watch for him, listen for him, and follow him in whatever challenges cross your path.

Where you have felt hopeless, may you discover the God of hope.

Where you have felt lonely, may you discover God-with-you.

Where you have felt anxious, may you discover the Prince of Peace.

And, finally, in words that Evelyn Underhill prayed over communities of men and women who came to retreats she often led:

O Lord Jesus Christ! Most blessed Lord! In whom is no variableness, neither shadow of turning, whose stillness is around and within us, the repose in the recollection of whose presence is joy and refreshment, enfold us in this ineffable peace, which is Your own unchanging will. Still our irritation. Soothe our restlessness: say to our hearts "Peace be still." Brood over us, within us, Spirit of perfect peace, so that outwardly we may reflect the inner stillness of our souls, and that we may bear change, anxiety, distractions, strains, disappointments, temptations and suffering and still be found confidently and peacefully in Your heart, O Jesus, enfolded in Your loving care. Let us in true quietness, fulfill the calling which is set before us. Be it even so, dear Lord, Amen.[1]

NON-ANXIOUS REFLECTION

- What has the "peace the world gives" looked like in your experience? How is it different from the peace God gives?

- What is surprising about the peace God gives? How do we become reshaped by God's way of peace?

- Does God's peace mean we never feel anxious? Why or why not? How do I measure my "peace levels"?

- How does numbing (and its cousins, escape and avoidance) counterfeit true soul rest? How do I tell the difference? How do I resist the temptation to numb, and enter instead into God-given rest?

ACKNOWLEDGMENTS

This book has been the hardest one to write so far. It took longer than I thought it would take. It has felt the most personal and often the most daunting. My sense of indebtedness to those who have prayed, encouraged, and helped me is great.

I want to thank especially those who have worked closely and fruitfully with me in my journey from anxiety to peace. I'm especially grateful for years of work with Dr. Ken Londeaux (1947–2022). If not for his helping me find freedom from paralyzing fear, anxiety, and depression, I would have never found the confidence or energy to write my first book, *An Unhurried Life*. That book has changed the course of my life. I continue to give thanks for the immeasurable grace God gave me through Dr. Ken.

I continue to be grateful for the team at InterVarsity Press. Their books have shaped my faith journey for decades. I am honored to be a part of their author community. I especially appreciate the help of Cindy Bunch and Nilwona Nowlin as my editors, and Lori Neff for her wise guidance and help in getting my books out there into the wide world. Thank you for giving this book a home from which to launch.

I continue to be grateful for the gift of our Unhurried Living team, board, donors, and other partners. We are thankful beyond measure for all the ways you've shared your talents, time, and resources to help fulfill this vision.

I am grateful for the partnership that Gem and I have enjoyed as husband and wife over the last thirty-eight years. These most recent ones have been perhaps the most collaborative and therefore fruitful. I've especially needed her encouragement and prayers over the course of this book's development. As always, "These two hearts never apart."

And, finally, to the Prince of Peace who has been mentoring me in his unhurried, non-anxious way, thank you. I'm so glad for your gifts of grace, mercy, hope, joy, and of course, peace. Thank you for the help of your Spirit in this work of writing. Apart from you, this book would not be possible. May you find pleasure and honor in this little offering.

Appendix A

A NON-ANXIOUS PRAYER

This is a personalized version of the prayer that closes the final chapter of this book. Offer it as a way of welcoming God's non-anxious presence to do his work of peace both in you and through you.

Father, thank you for the peace I can find in being chosen by you. How good to grow confident that you enjoy being with me. Thank you for all the good things you have prepared in advance for me to enjoy and to share with others. Grant that my life would become so full of your goodness and grace that I would overflow for the good of others. May I learn in that way to work hard without working hurried.

Show me how to work closely with you, Father, rather than serving you at a distance. Enable me to be active without being hyperactive. Teach me to work at the pace of relationship, at the pace of love. Give me eyes to see the people under whom, alongside whom, and for whom I serve.

Guide me in the ways of fruitfulness that are productivity at the pace of peace. Protect me from the temptation to be driven by anxious activity. I want to learn how to join Jesus in the very fruitful work he is already doing in and around me. May I grow in working hard at the pace of grace rather than working frantically at the pace of driven achievement. Help me to walk in the presence of grace rather than outrunning grace. May your Spirit empower me to follow grace, to be strengthened by grace, and to walk in grace.

When I am tempted to believe that this peaceful, non-anxious way of living and working is impossible because of my current situation, grant me a clearer vision of Jesus' holy and unhurried way of living and leading that is present with me now. Grow my discernment so that I learn how to walk with Jesus rather than hurrying ahead of Jesus. Show me how to live and work at the pace of abiding in Christ. May this depth result in far greater fruit than frantic busyness will ever produce.

Grant me a steady, calm vision of Jesus, *the* non-anxious One with me. Grow in me patience to watch for him, listen for him, and follow him in whatever challenges cross my path.

When I feel hopeless, help me remember the God of hope with me.

When I feel lonely, help me know the presence of God-with-me.

When I feel anxious, remind me that the Prince of Peace is with me in this very moment.

O God, you never change. You are always a bright light in my darkness, sure hope in my despair, deep peace in my anxious worry. In your stillness, I find joy and refreshment. Speak words of love and calm over me in this moment. Give me ears to hear you speak to the storm of my emotions, "Peace. Be still." May your Spirit of perfect peace reign in my mind, my heart, my body.

May my visible life bear the outward fruit of my soul growing in peace. Strengthen me with joy and peace so that I can bear up under whatever change, cares, distractions, stresses, disappointments, or temptations may cross my path. In these trying situations, may my soul find itself at home in your loving care. Grant me a heart of peace as I step out to do the work you've given me to do. May you do all this and more, in the name of the God of peace. Amen.

Appendix B

GROUP GUIDE

The guide below is designed for a seven-session small group or leadership team experience. In preparation for each meeting, participants will read two chapters and spend some time with the non-anxious reflection questions at the end of each chapter. This guide assumes each gathering of the group will be about one hour.

PREPARATION FOR MEETING ONE

Read chapters one and two.

- Reflect on the non-anxious reflection questions for these chapters.
- Reflect on how to share your own journey with anxiety with the others in your group.

MEETING ONE

Open your meeting in prayer, welcoming the Prince of Peace among you. Invite God's peace to be very present in each of you and among you as you meet.

Share with one another what was helpful or challenging from the two chapters or the reflection questions. Seek to be fully engaged as you listen to others share.

At the end of chapter two, the first reflection question invites readers to spend five minutes in silence. If you are willing to try that together, have one member of the group set a five-minute timer. Imagine you are sitting in a serene cathedral together. At the end of the five minutes, describe what your experience was like.

Also at the end of chapter two, the third reflection question might be a good way to close your gathering. If you've been able to share some of the "what ifs" that arise in your lives these days, take time to offer those to God prayerfully. Invite God's peace to guard your thoughts and emotions going forward.

PREPARATION FOR MEETING TWO

Read chapters three and four.

- Reflect on the non-anxious reflection questions for these chapters.
- Come prepared to share how something from your reading intersected with your life experience.

MEETING TWO

Open your meeting in prayer, welcoming the Prince of Peace among you. Invite God's peace to be very present in each of you and among you as you meet.

Share with one another what was helpful or challenging from the two chapters or the reflection questions. Share how something from your reading intersected with your life experience.

You might close your gathering with a prayer rooted in Paul's message of grace that begins and ends his letters. Something like, "Grace to you and peace from God our Father and the Lord Jesus Christ."

PREPARATION FOR MEETING THREE

Read chapters five and six.

- Reflect on the non-anxious reflection questions for those chapters.

- Come prepared to share how something from your reading intersected with your life experience.

MEETING THREE

Open your meeting in prayer, welcoming the Prince of Peace among you. Allow a few moments of quiet for personal reflection and welcome of God's presence.

Share with one another what was helpful or challenging from the two chapters or the reflection questions. How is God speaking to places of anxiety in your life through what you're reading?

Close your time prayerfully. What do you want to thank God for? What do you appreciate about who God is and how God is with you? What help do you want to ask for?

PREPARATION FOR MEETING FOUR

Read chapters seven and eight.

- Reflect on the non-anxious reflection questions for those chapters.

- Come prepared to share how something from your reading intersected with your life experience.

MEETING FOUR

Open your meeting in prayer, welcoming the Prince of Peace among you. As hope is one of our themes for this meeting, take time to acknowledge God among you as the God of hope.

Offer thanks for the good path ahead that God is preparing for each one.

Share with one another what was helpful or challenging from the two chapters or the reflection questions. How is God speaking to places of anxiety in your life through what you're reading?

Close your time prayerfully. What do you want to thank God for? What do you appreciate about who God is and how God is with you? What help do you want to ask for?

PREPARATION FOR MEETING FIVE

Read chapters nine and ten.

- Reflect on the non-anxious reflection questions for those chapters.

- Come prepared to share something from your reading that spoke to where you find yourself these days.

MEETING FIVE

Open your meeting in prayer, welcoming the Prince of Peace among you. Invite God's peace to be very present in each of you and among you as you meet.

Both chapters speak to finding peace in places of challenge and difficulty. As you share with one another, be as honest as you are able about hard places you are currently facing. Listen to one another with grace and compassion.

Share with one another what was helpful or challenging from the two chapters or the reflection questions. How is God speaking peace in the hard places of your life through what you're reading?

Close your time prayerfully. Where do you feel need for God's peace to come and care for you? For what might you thank God? Where do you need help?

PREPARATION FOR MEETING SIX

Read chapters eleven and twelve.

- ◆ Reflect on the non-anxious reflection questions for those chapters.

- ◆ Come prepared to share something from your reading that spoke to where you find yourself these days.

MEETING SIX

Open your meeting in prayer, welcoming the Prince of Peace among you. Invite God's peace to be very present in each of you and among you as you meet.

Share with one another what you found helpful or challenging from the two chapters or the reflection questions. What is happening in your experience of worry and your experience of peace in this reading journey?

Take a moment to share any invitations from God you've been sensing along the way. In what ways is God inviting you to a journey of transformation from an anxious life to a more non-anxious life?

Close your time prayerfully. Where do you feel need for God's peace to come and care for you? For what might you thank God? Where do you need help?

PREPARATION FOR MEETING SEVEN

Read chapters thirteen and fourteen.

- ◆ Reflect on the non-anxious reflection questions for those chapters.

- ◆ Come prepared to share something from your reading that spoke to where you find yourself these days.

MEETING SEVEN

Open your meeting in prayer, welcoming the Prince of Peace among you. Invite God's peace to be very present in each of you and among you as you meet.

In this last gathering, continue to share with one another what you found helpful or challenging from the two chapters or the reflection questions.

Allow a bit of time to reflect aloud together about how God has been at work in and among you over these seven meetings. What have been some of God's gifts to you on this journey you've been on together? Share with one another and be thankful together.

You could close this gathering with the non-anxious prayer in the appendixes. Whether you read it aloud together, read it silently, or have one in your group pray it on your behalf, welcome the gracious peace God wishes to give you in prayer.

NOTES

1. BECOMING A MASTER OF ANXIETY

[1]Renee D. Goodwin et al., "Trends in Anxiety Among Young Adults in the United States, 2008-2018: Rapid Increases Among Young Adults," National Library of Medicine, August 21, 2020, www.ncbi.nlm.nih.gov/pmc/articles /PMC7441973/.

[2]World Health Organization, "COVID-19 Pandemic Triggers 25% Increase in Prevalence of Anxiety and Depression Worldwide," March 2, 2022, www .who.int/news/item/02-03-2022-covid-19-pandemic-triggers-25-increase -in-prevalence-of-anxiety-and-depression-worldwide.

3. STUDENTS BECOME MENTORS

[1]John Cassian, *Conferences,* trans. Colm Luibheid (New York: Paulist Press, 1985), 20.

4. GRACIOUS FULLNESS

[1]I first heard Wayne Anderson share these insights in a presentation to the alumni of The Leadership Institute in Orange, California, on February 7, 1994.

[2]"The grace of the/our Lord Jesus be with you [all]" (Romans 16:20; 1 Corinthians 16:23; 1 Thessalonians 5:28; 2 Thessalonians 3:18). "The grace of the Lord Jesus Christ and the love of God and the fellowship of the Holy Spirit be with you all" (2 Corinthians 13:14). "The grace of our Lord Jesus Christ be with your spirit, [brothers. Amen]" (Galatians 6:18; Philemon 25). "Grace be with all who love our Lord Jesus Christ with love incorruptible" (Ephesians 6:24). "The grace of our Lord Jesus Christ be with your spirit" (Philippians 4:23). "Grace be with you [all]" (Colossians 4:18; 1 Timothy 6:21; 2 Timothy 4:22; Titus 3:15; Hebrews 13:25).

[3]"Grace and peace to you from God our Father and from the Lord Jesus Christ" (Romans 1:7; 1 Corinthians 1:3; 2 Corinthians 1:2; Galatians 1:3;

Ephesians 1:2; Philippians 1:2; Colossians 1:2; 2 Thessalonians 1:2; Philemon 3). "Grace and peace to you" (1 Thessalonians 1:1). "Grace, mercy and peace from God the Father and Christ Jesus our Lord" (1 Timothy 1:2; 2 Timothy 1:2). "Grace and peace from God the Father and Christ Jesus our Savior" (Titus 1:4).

[4]"Scrupulosity," Wikipedia, accessed April 27, 2023, https://en.wikipedia.org/wiki/Scrupulosity.

[5]Alan Fadling, *An Unhurried Leader* (Downers Grove, IL: InterVarsity Press, 2017), 54.

5. PRACTICING PRESENCE

[1]Brother Lawrence, *The Practice of the Presence of God*, revised and rewritten by Harold J. Chadwick (North Brunswick, NJ: Bridge-Logos Publishers, 1999).

[2]Thomas H. Green, *The Friend of the Bridegroom* (Notre Dame, IN: Ave Maria Press, 2000), 43.

[3]Gerald May, *The Wisdom of Wilderness* (San Francisco: HarperSanFrancisco, 2006), 143.

6. SIMPLE VIRTUES

[1]Wendy Wright, *Heart Speaks to Heart: The Salesian Tradition* (Maryknoll, NY: Orbis Books, 2004), 55-56.

[2]Saint Mark the Ascetic, "On Those That Think That They Are Made Righteous by Works," in *The Philokalia, Volume 1*, trans. and ed. G. E. H. Palmer, Philip Sherrard, and Kallistos Ware (Boston: Faber and Faber, 1979), 134.

[3]Saint Mark the Ascetic, "On Those That Think That They are Made Righteous," 134.

[4]Francis de Sales, *Introduction to the Devout Life*, trans. John K. Ryan (New York: Image Books/Doubleday, 1972), 150.

[5]You'll find a lot of help here in Cindy Bunch, *Be Kind to Yourself* (Downers Grove, IL: InterVarsity Press, 2020).

[6]Wendy Wright, *Heart Speaks to Heart*, 33.

[7]Francis de Sales and Jane de Chantal, *Letters of Spiritual Direction*, trans. Pérrone Marie Thibert (Mahwah, NJ: Paulist Press, 1988), 152.

7. UNEXPECTED PATHS TO PEACE

[1]Francis de Sales and Jane de Chantal, *Letters of Spiritual Direction*, trans. Péronne Marie Thibert (New York: Paulist Press, 1988), 194.

[2]Thomas Merton, *The Hidden Ground of Love*, ed. William Shannon (New York: Farrar, Strauss & Giroux, 1985), 375.

[3]de Sales and de Chantal, *Letters of Spiritual Direction*, 232.

[4]David Benner, *Surrender to Love* (Downers Grove, IL: InterVarsity Press, 2003), 91.

[5]Saint Benedict, *The Rule of St. Benedict in English*, ed. Timothy Fry (Collegeville, MN: The Liturgical Press, 1982), 28.

[6]Saint Hesychios the Priest, "On Watchfulness and Holiness: St. Mark the Ascetic," in *The Philokalia, Volume 1*, trans. and ed. G. E. H. Palmer, Philip Sherrard, and Kallistos Ware (Boston: Faber and Faber, 1979), 164-65.

8. A BUOYANT LIFE

[1]Dallas Willard, *The Divine Conspiracy* (San Francisco: HarperSanFrancisco, 1998), 62. Gem and I have written on the theme of joy in our book, *What Does Your Soul Love?* (Downers Grove, IL: InterVarsity Press, 2019), 151-68.

9. CONFRONTING THE GIANT

[1]Eugene Peterson, *Leap Over a Wall* (San Francisco: HarperSanFrancisco, 1997), 39.

[2]Peterson, *Leap Over a Wall*, 39-40.

[3]Adapted from Alan Fadling, "Managing Our Omnipresent Smartphones," December 2, 2019, in *The Unhurried Living Podcast*, www.unhurriedliving.com/blog/podcast103/.

10. PEACE IN TROUBLING TIMES

[1]I owe a great debt to Dr. Ken Londeaux (1947–2022), a counselor with whom I worked for years on my anxiety and depression, and without whom I would never have found the courage to write my first book, *An Unhurried Life*.

11. EMBODIED PEACE

[1]Martin Laird, *Into the Silent Land* (New York: Oxford University Press, 2006), 16.

[2]James K. A. Smith, *You Are What You Love* (Grand Rapids, MI: Brazos Press, 2016), 3.

[3]Gerald May, *The Wisdom of Wilderness* (San Francisco: HarperSanFrancisco, 2006), 45.

12. RHYTHMS OF PEACE

[1]This passage is adapted from Alan Fadling, "Six Practices for Spiritual Retreat," from the *Unhurried Living* blog, June 15, 2022, www.unhurried living.com/blog/spiritual-retreat.

[2]Esther de Waal, *The Celtic Way of Prayer* (New York: Doubleday, 1997), 109.

13. NON-ANXIOUS WORK

[1]Abbé Huvelin, *Some Spiritual Guides of the Seventeenth Century*, trans. Rev. Joseph Leonard (New York: Benziger Brothers, 1927), 112.

[2]Alan Fadling, *An Unhurried Life* (Downers Grove, IL: InterVarsity Press, 2020), 127.

[3]Edwin Friedman, *A Failure of Nerve* (New York: Church Publishing, 2017), 23.

[4]Thomas H. Green, *A Friend of the Bridegroom* (Notre Dame, IN: Ave Maria Press, 2000), 43.

[5]Evelyn Underhill, *Evelyn Underhill's Prayer Book*, ed. Robin Wrigley-Carr (London: SPCK, 2018), 56.

14. BECOMING A MASTER OF PEACE

[1]Evelyn Underhill, *Evelyn Underhill's Prayer Book*, ed. Robin Wrigley-Carr (London: SPCK, 2018), 90.

 unhurried**living**

Many leaders feel hurried, and hurry is costing them more than they realize. Unhurried Living, founded by Alan and Gem Fadling, provides coaching, resources, and training to help people learn to lead from fullness rather than leading on empty.

Busy is a matter of calendar. Hurry is a matter of soul.

Built on more than thirty years of experience at the intersection of spiritual formation and leadership development, Unhurried Living seeks to inspire Christian leaders around the world to rest deeper so they can live fuller and lead better.

Spiritual leadership is the influence that grows in the life of a leader being transformed by the power of God's Spirit. Spiritual leadership is learning to robustly practice spiritual disciplines that deepen the roots of leaders in the love of God.

Effective spiritual leaders learn to experience the depths of God's love so they know how to lead others into those same depths. Such leadership bears the fruit of transformed lives and expanded kingdom influence.

We seek to respond to questions many are asking:

Rest deeper: Why do I so often feel more drained than energized? Can I find space for my soul to breathe?

Live fuller: I have tried to fill my life with achievements, possessions, and popularity, and I feel emptier than ever. Where can I find fullness that lasts?

Lead better: How can I step off the treadmill of mere busyness and make real, meaningful progress in my life and work?

Rediscover the genius of Jesus' unhurried way of life and leadership.

Come visit us at unhurriedliving.com to discover free resources to help you

Rest Deeper. Live Fuller. Lead Better.

Web: unhurriedliving.com
Facebook: facebook.com/unhurriedliving
Instagram: UnhurriedLiving
Email: info@unhurriedliving.com

Also Available from Unhurried Living

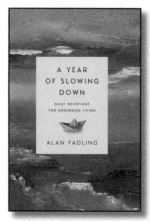

A Year of Slowing Down
978-1-5140-0318-3

Hold That Thought
978-0-8308-3169-2

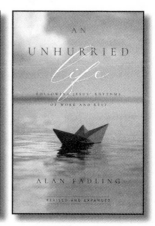

An Unhurried Life
978-0-8308-4672-6

What Does Your Soul Love?
978-0-8308-4659-7

An Unhurried Leader
978-0-8308-4631-3